BUSINESS WRITING
THAT WORKS!

Cynthia Lynch Bischoff

Business Writing Consultant and Trainer

White Raven Press
Norfolk, Virginia

PREFACE

Since 1982, I have trained thousands of business people to write effectively. My workshop **Business Writing That Works!** has been a bridge for many people to gain critical skills in getting started in writing, choosing the right words, watching their tone and style, writing effective letters and memos, and knowing where to put the comma. I am happy to say that these workshops have received consistently excellent reviews and have been highly praised for providing practical, immediate help with everyday writing tasks. In fact, participants have frequently asked me when I would be writing a desk reference based on my workshop principles. This book is an answer to those requests and is designed to present information that is needed to write effectively.

I have taken great care to write this book in a "user-friendly" style that will benefit both new and experienced writers. Even though my workshop participants had varied abilities and needs, I found that most of them expressed the same general feelings.

- They felt that the training that they had received in high school and college had not prepared them well for writing on the job (for example, an essay is not a letter);

- They compensated for their lack of training by going through files and trying to imitate what others had done with usually unsatisfactory results.

This book will take you step by step through the writing process and will help you to understand the importance of all facets of business writing. Formulas, writing tips, and exercises will empower you to put across your ideas quickly, concisely, and confidently.

Key Features of the Book

You will find the organization and format of this book easy to follow. The formats of individual chapters vary for chapter content, but throughout the book, the goal has been to provide a concise presentation of the most important writing concepts, along with real-life examples and opportunities for practice.

This book functions both as a tutorial and as a quick reference guide. If you routinely have difficulty with most of your writing tasks, it would probably be most helpful to read the book chapter by chapter. By doing so, you will be gaining progressive skills in learning to write well. However, you will find the book equally useful as a quick reference to locate answers to questions about letter and memo formats, grammar corrections, or usage choices.

ACKNOWLEDGMENTS

To the many students in my workshops and courses in business writing, I thank you for your suggestions and feedback in helping me to shape a book that would best serve all business writers.

I extend a special thanks to my friends and colleagues, Mona Danner, Kim Fisher, Michelle Kelley, and Rick Corbin and the Quest for Excellence crew. Your heartfelt encouragement motivated me to create this book from my workshop material.

To my co-workers, Fleta Jackson, Claudette Johnson, and James Patrick, I greatly appreciate your daily support in helping me to meet my goals.

I am especially grateful to Col. Robert Flanagan and Liz Witkowski for their assistance in the design and production of this book and cover. I have certainly appreciated your cheerful attitude and patience. You both spent countless hours in making this book possible, and I sincerely thank you.

To my children, Matthew and Courtney, I thank you for your remarkable patience and love during the great many hours I spent writing, especially when I know you wanted to use the computer for video games. You have been, and always will be, an inspiration to me.

Finally, to my husband Bruce, I offer sincere thanks and love for your incredible patience and support. You spent great amounts of your personal time helping me to format the book and manage the computer issues, provided excellent feedback on the material (always playing the role of the writer "who might not know"), and were consistently there for me in all aspects of my work—physically, emotionally, and spiritually.

Contents

CHAPTER 1

Writing Is a Process, Not Just a Product

D o you recall the last writing class you attended, whether in high school or college? A typical writing assignment is to compose an essay. Just as typical is for the teacher to select a specific length for the essay, usually 500 words. Even if you had a certain topic in mind and a purpose established, what did you find yourself focusing on? Yes, the 500 words.

Too often, business people report that their high school and college teachers encouraged them to increase their sentence length and to use "bigger" words. That is the usual academic style, and in a school setting, it can lead to success.

In contrast, in the business world, clients, co-workers, and supervisors want you to get to the point, to say it as succinctly as possible, and to be specific. In business, *time is money*. Even if you have a good idea, if your message is too long or too hard to read, no one will read it.

Often in my workshops, people say that they left school and entered the workplace still writing for a teacher who is no longer there. The first step in effective business writing, then, is to understand that you have an actual **audience** (not a teacher). The second is to recognize the impact of your **tone** and **style** on the message itself. The third step is to choose an appropriate **format** (or order for the message). The fourth is to maintain **writer credibility**—the appropriate use of grammar, mechanics, and word choice.

The foundation for understanding and applying these four critical steps is to recognize that writing is a *process*, not just a *product*. If, for example, you focus on the way your memo will look in final form rather than on the stages needed to state the message clearly, then you are focusing on product rather than process, and it is likely that you will not communicate effectively. Another frequent outcome of focusing on product is a feeling of writer's block (or the inability for the writer to proceed).

In this chapter we will focus on the four stages of the writing process and will discuss techniques related to each of the four stages:

Stage 1: **Prewriting**
(Getting Ideas Started)

Stage 2: **Writing**
(Drafting the Message)

Stage 3: **Revising**
(Changing the Message)

Stage 4: **Editing**
(Proofreading)

Stage 1: Prewriting

Brainstorming

Effective writers think about how to write before they begin. They make plans. There are varying tools that effective writers use to get started. The most typical tool is **brainstorming**. In brainstorming, you may begin by thinking about your topic (for example, the memo to your boss to request vacation), and then quickly jot down your ideas as they occur to you. Don't stop to analyze your writing at this stage; just continue to write until you run out of ideas. Such a list might look like the example in Figure 1.

Figure 1: Brainstorming

Memo to Boss re: Vacation

Need December 20-28

Busy time for the office

Worked last year over the entire break

Have seniority over current staff

Will be going out of town so need more travel time

Am willing to work New Year's eve and day

Sally has taken off a week at Christmas for 3 yrs now

Outlining

After listing your ideas, you could then organize them into a format that would be appropriate. For example, you may decide to create an **outline,** another type of prewriting technique. An informal outline allows you to create a simple list marked with bullets, symbols, or codes that might indicate the importance among ideas. If you outline the same ideas generated above, your outline might appear as shown in Figure 2.

Notice that in outlining, the focus is on *ordering the information* in the way that it will be presented in the actual memo. Brainstorming may be helpful as a first activity before outlining since the focus of brainstorming is to *generate ideas,* with little or no emphasis on order.

When you outline, be sure to work with a comfortable outline format. Again, in our academic training, we may have learned the Roman numeral system (i.e., if I have an "A," I need a "B," etc.). Did you ever create a "B" simply because you were supposed to have it, even though you didn't need that information? For most writers simple bullet points or Arabic numbers (1, 2, 3. . .) are easier to use. Work to find your own method.

Figure 2: Outlining

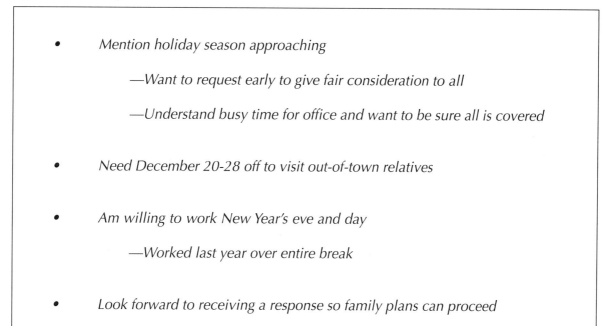

- *Mention holiday season approaching*

    —Want to request early to give fair consideration to all

    —Understand busy time for office and want to be sure all is covered

- *Need December 20-28 off to visit out-of-town relatives*

- *Am willing to work New Year's eve and day*

    —Worked last year over entire break

- *Look forward to receiving a response so family plans can proceed*

Stage 1: Prewriting (cont'd)

Mapping

Another type of prewriting activity is **mapping**. This type of prewriting technique is strong visually. In elementary school through college, writers often call this type of prewriting "creating a web." The writer begins by creating a circle on the page with the main topic in the circle. As ideas come to the writer, he or she continues to *map* out the ideas or build a *web*. An example of a web for the earlier memo task can be seen in Figure 3. Notice that relationships of ideas are indicated by the placement within the web.

Figure 3: Mapping

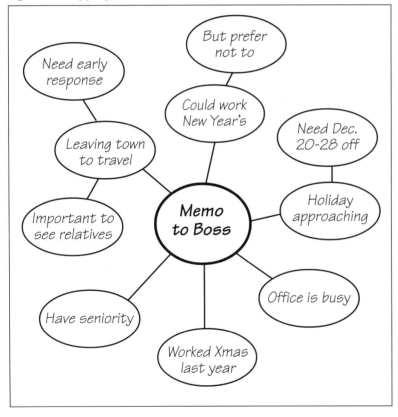

Freewriting

A fourth type of prewriting is **freewriting**, a technique that involves writing spontaneously for brief, sustained periods of ten or fifteen minutes. Freewriting can remain *unfocused* if you are searching for a topic or ideas or *focused* if you know the topic but are deciding how to approach it.

Freewriting focuses on writing complete sentences during this specific time constraint, allowing the writer to focus on content rather than on correctness. In this process, you will write quickly whatever comes to your mind. Do not worry about grammar, spelling, neatness, and so on. Simply write! If you cannot think of something to say, write "I cannot think of anything to say" until another thought comes to you. Since you will resist writing the "I cannot" statement, other ideas will come to you.

This technique works very well for writers who feel blocked or unable to begin the writing process. Figure 4 offers an example of freewriting on the original vacation memo topic.

Figure 4: Freewriting

I need to write a memo to Rebecca.

I hate writing this. Okay, in December I have to visit Mom in Indiana so
I'm going to need to take off December 20-28.
That allows for enough travel time.
When are the kids off from school for the holidays?
I'd better check that out tomorrow.
Last year I worked through the break but I owe it to myself and
the kids to visit this year.
Going out of town would be something R understands since after all her
folks are from Nevada.
I could work New Year's Day to make up the time.
Should I bargain with this point or just wait for her response. . . ?

Journalists' Questions

A fifth type of prewriting technique is using ***Journalists' Questions***.

Journalists have long used a set of reliable questions to investigate the writing task: *who, what, when, where, why,* and *how*. Asking these questions during your initial writing stage can help you to explore your topic and your audience fully. A sample of journalists' questions that writers ask is found in Chapter 3 on Audience (Figure 9).

Stage 2: Writing

Writing a draft – the second stage of the writing process – is somewhat like a rehearsal. It is an opportunity to get the ideas flowing into a specific order and to explore possible expression. During the prewriting stage, you were formulating ideas and trying to achieve focus. In **Stage 2-Writing**, you are allowing the ideas to begin to take shape as a product – the letter, memo, or report. You may write with your brainstorming or your web in front of you, or you may simply work from the outline you may have created in your prewriting.

Whatever your method, it is essential in the writing stage to allow yourself to write freely without worrying about grammar, mechanics, or neatness. It is more important to get the ideas down.

Writing at this stage requires careful thinking, planning, and analyzing. It helps to keep a few general guidelines in place during this stage. See Figure 5.

Figure 5: General Guidelines for Stage 2—Writing

Remember your audience. *Remember that you have a reader or readers in mind. How are you meeting the needs of the reader(s)?*

Remember your purpose. *What point are you trying to make?*

Gather the information and materials you need. *Keep yourself from getting distracted since you break your train of thought to search for items. Accessibility saves time.*

Don't worry about troublesome sections. *Be flexible and allow yourself to make changes as needed. This isn't the final stage of your writing. Expect to rewrite as needed.*

Periodically give yourself a break from writing if the task is long. *While too many interruptions can create inconsistencies, it is helpful occasionally to get away from your writing to maintain objectivity and a fresh perspective.*

Stage 3: Revising

Only very talented and very naïve writers create a final product in the second stage of the process. For most of us, the second stage often blends into the third stage – that of **revising**. Revising involves rethinking, reorganizing, and refining the draft. Revision may involve changing content and altering tone or style. As you revise, let the guidelines in Figure 6 lead you.

Figure 6: General Guidelines for Stage 3–Revising

__Set aside your first draft for as long as possible.__ Your goal is to gain some objectivity. Often setting aside a document for even fifteen minutes can allow you to spot an inconsistency or to feel the document tone differently.

__Check the document for whether or not it has met your intended goal.__ Did you respond to your audience in an appropriate way? Were you able to meet the reader's and your own needs?

__Check the tone and style for effectiveness.__   What is your attitude in this piece (your tone)? Are you clear and succinct without sounding choppy (your style)?

__Check the content of your writing for accuracy.__ Is your content clear? Is there enough detail or too much? Are the facts accurate, for example, the date, time, and location of the meeting?

__Ask others for feedback.__   If you are at all unsure of the effect of your writing or the specifics of your content, ask others for feedback. Perhaps you can establish a working writing relationship with a co-worker whose opinion you trust. Networking in writing is as important as any business networking.

Stage 4: Editing/Proofreading

The final stage of the writing process focuses on correction and presentation of an overall perfect copy. Remember that your reputation depends often upon your written product. This is what we referred to earlier as "writer credibility." It is critical to allow yourself some time away from the document before attempting this final stage. (Time away from the document may vary from five minutes to two days depending upon the complexity of the document.) It may be helpful to edit your own work several times or to ask for someone else to glance over your final draft.

Since the writing process is recursive (i.e., the stages can loop back on each other), you may find sections in the fourth stage that require that you return to the revision stage. As you edit your work, ask yourself the questions in Figure 7. (Later chapters also provide critical material related to this stage of writing.)

Figure 7: General Guidelines for Stage 4—Editing/Proofreading

---

Are all sentences complete? *While occasionally we choose to include a desirable fragment (a part of a sentence) in our work, in most business documents, we want to strive for complete sentences.*

Are all words spelled correctly? *Use Spellchecker, or check a dictionary for questionable words.*

Is usage correctly employed? *Remember that Spellchecker does not correct errors involving incorrectly used word choices – for example, "affect" and "effect." See Chapter 8 for further information.*

Are any necessary words omitted? *Are any words unnecessarily repeated?*

Do subjects and verbs as well as nouns and pronouns agree in number? *See Chapter 9 for useful information.*

Are sentences mechanically and structurally correct? *See Chapter 9 for useful information.*

Take your time and check your work carefully.

If you need to make a correction on the computer, glance through the entire work <u>after</u> it is printed to be sure that correcting one error does not create another.

Be sure that your final product is neat, clean, and visually pleasing. *You never have a second chance to make a first impression.*

Above all, remember that *writer credibility equals professional credibility.* In other words, if you send a memo that contains a spelling or word choice error, your credibility as a writer is affected. In addition, your professional credibility may be judged since the reader may consider you to be careless or less knowledgeable.

Writing Exercises

(To practice prewriting skills, you may attempt to perform the exercises in Appendix C, and check possible answers in Appendix D.)

Basic Characteristics of Business Writing

L et's go back to those high school and college classes. We discussed in Chapter 1 the writing of the 500-word essay, and we mentioned that teachers often asked us to increase our sentence length and word level. We also noted that the business world asks for short and clear writing. What are other differences between academic and professional writing?

In my workshop, I teach five critical characteristics of professional writing. "Professional writing" here is used as a larger umbrella term to cover business, management, technical writing, and so on.

Five Critical Characteristics of Business Writing

The five characteristics of business writing include *audience, tone, style, format,* and *writer credibility.*

A brief description of each characteristic is found in this chapter; however, a chapter is devoted to each of these components. I believe that a clear understanding of each of these characteristics is necessary for a person to be an effective business writer.

Audience

The *audience* is the specific receiver of your message. As a sender of information, whether written or spoken, you have an intended receiver. *Who* is this person or these people? Knowing your audience members and carefully analyzing their needs is critical to business writing success. Lack of knowledge of your reader is similar to trying to sell a product and not knowing anything about the buyer. *Know your audience.* (Chapter 3 focuses on audience.)

Tone

The *tone* is the "attitude" that your writing suggests, and believe me, all writing expresses the writer's attitude! The attitude may be business-like, appropriate, curt, angry, even arrogant – but there is an attitude. Attitude is created from the words that you choose.

Four key elements of tone are critical in business writing. In most workplace writing, you want your tone to be *natural, tactful, personal,* and *positive.* The elements of effective customer service can be applied to effective writing. Know your audience and write with an appropriate and respectful tone. (Chapter 4 focuses on tone.)

Style

While your word choices reflect the tone or attitude in your writing, your *style* is reflected by the length and structure of your sentences. Do you have a flowery style (one that is characterized by long sentences and phrases instead of strong action words)? Or is your style succinct but bordering on choppy?

What effect do you wish to have? How do you want your writing to "sound"? Paying attention to sentence structure involves understanding your intent and learning how to achieve it. (Chapter 5 provides practical information on how to create an effective style.)

Format

In stage 2 of the writing process – writing – discussed in Chapter 1, you learned that the order of the message or its *format* is critical to getting your message read.

Do you write letters and memos that are ignored because of length or complexity of the material? Do you desire a way to write e-mail messages that helps insure that your message will be read and not overlooked as one of a large number of messages? Read Chapters 6 and 7 on choosing the appropriate format to get your message across.

Writer Credibility

If you send a letter to a client and that letter contains a typo, a usage error, or an ambiguous phrase, what is the impression you give? It is doubtful that the client will say, "Oh, well, I guess Joe was rushed yesterday." Instead, the client, like most people, is likely to associate writing credibility with professional credibility. The error will reflect poorly on you as a writer and as a professional. More than likely, the client may associate the writing error with general carelessness.

Chapters 8 and 9 focus on usage, grammar, and mechanics in an attempt to help you to maintain writer credibility.

CHAPTER 3

Consider Your Audience

Formula:

"I am writing this for _____ because I want to _____."

While this formula is quite simple, it always works to get you focused. It also places your reader at the forefront of your process. I recommend using it to focus every business writing activity.

Remember that in business your writing is not graded by the teacher but by your audience. Who are your readers now? How does one reader differ from another and therefore require something different from you as a writer?

Effective writers focus on the audience. Since the goal of any successful communication venture is shared meaning between sender and receiver, it is important to pay attention to the receiver of the message. Instead of being "writer-centered" or concentrating on their own needs, effective business writers are "reader-centered." They attempt to meet the reader's needs and in turn to establish shared meaning. It is not that the reader's needs are met at the expense of the writer's needs. Rather, the goal is for both needs to be met.

To begin being "reader-centered," understand that in business there are varied audiences. In fact, most of the management writing teachers I know acknowledge that four levels, or categories, of audience exist. These categories of readers are distinguished by the audience's knowledge of generalized and specialized vocabulary. **Generalized vocabulary** refers to words that are general in nature and not specific to a certain occupation. Examples might include words like *pay* or *compensation*. While *pay* would be considered *low-level* generalized vocabulary since most people would understand it, *compensation* would be *high-level* generalized. **Specialized vocabulary** refers to words that are specific to a certain discipline or field of study (e.g., medicine, engineering, or accounting terms), words like *hematoma* or *abaxial*.

Figure 8 provides a chart of the four levels of audience. It will help you to categorize the different types of audience members you may serve. Figure 8 is followed by an explanation of the different levels.

Figure 8: Levels of Audience

Levels of Audience	Knowledge of High-level **Generalized** Vocabulary	**Specialized** Vocabulary
Expert	X	X
Executive	X	
Skilled Worker		X
Layperson		
	KEY: X = Has Knowledge	

Audience Members

Figure 8 shows four audience levels. These four levels describe stereotypes of reader categories, and there will be exceptions to each general category. It is helpful, though, to use these categories as a basis for viewing the different business audiences you may serve.

The **Expert** is a term usually applied to a person with expert content knowledge in a specialized area that is the subject of the writing. For example, a doctor or nurse might qualify as a medical expert if the topic is medicine. This person usually has a college education. For this reason, the chart indicates that this audience member who is educated will probably have knowledge of high-level generalized vocabulary (able to use words like *compensation* instead of *pay*) and will also have knowledge of specialized terms or what is often referred to as "content jargon."

If you are an expert, writing for another expert may be similar to writing for yourself.

The **Executive** refers to an individual who has a college degree in a field of study but who does not have a degree in the specific discipline of your writing. In other words, if you are an expert in a medical setting and you are writing about a medical illness, an executive could be represented by the hospital personnel director or quality assurance manager – a person who certainly has expert knowledge in a given field, but not in the field about which you are writing.

The executive would understand highly generalized vocabulary as indicated in Figure 8 but may not have knowledge of the specialized vocabulary being used. Often in our businesses, we find ourselves writing for the executive who might be a coworker but someone in a different department. It is particularly important to pay attention to the acronyms that we might use freely with the expert.

The **Skilled Worker** is an individual who may have little or no formal training in a specific field of study; however, that person does have on-the-job training and experience. This person, for example, in our medical analogy, may be a nurse's aide or orderly. The person may not understand your highly generalized vocabulary but may understand the specialized terms used due to experience in working with those terms.

The **Layperson** is a person regarded as a general audience member. We cannot be sure that this person is highly educated both in a general or a specific sense in regard to our use of vocabulary. We evaluate this individual based on our general understanding of the public. Certainly we can make adjustments as needed as we write.

What is the average reading level in the United States today? If you answered seventh grade level, you would be accurate. When writing for a lay audience it is critical to understand the needs of the layperson in regard to use of vocabulary.

Remember that communication is the sending and receiving of information with the intent of achieving *shared meaning*. Our goal is to be understood which may require that we analyze the audience closely.

Analyzing the Audience

Now that we have established that varied levels of receivers exist for our information, we realize that it is critical to ask questions about our audience. Figure 9 is a chart of sample questions for writers to ask. You may come up with additional questions to fit your writing situation.

Figure 9: Sample Questions for Writers to Ask

WHO?
Who is my reader?
Who does my reader think I am?

WHAT?
What does my reader have or know already?
What does my reader need to know about this subject?
What will interest my reader? —not interest my reader?
What will help my reader to understand this subject?
What does my reader expect of me?
What is my reader's educational and/or socio-economic background?
What are my reader's attitudes and opinions?
What terms do I need to be sure the reader understands?
What message do I wish to convey?

WHEN?
When does my reader need this information?
When do I want a reply from my reader?
When will the event about which I'm writing (for example, the meeting) take place?
When should I begin this writing project? When is it due?

WHERE?
Where can I get the information my reader needs or wants?
Where do my reader's attitudes and opinions come from?
Where is the event taking place and at what time and location?

WHY?
Why is this subject and task important to me and my goals?
Why is this subject important to my reader?
Why should this reader pay attention to me?
Why should this reader NOT pay attention to me?
Why does this reader need this information?
Why is my reader interested in this subject?
Why is my reader NOT interested in this subject?

HOW?
How much information does my reader need?
How much time and effort am I asking from my reader?
How much time and effort will my reader give me?
How can I help the reader to understand the subject?
How can I show my reader what we have in common?
How does my reader feel about this subject?
How can I best provide shared meaning?

Note that these questions cover two basic areas of information that effective business writers seek to know about their audiences: **demographics** and **psychographics**. Demographics refers to the "hard data": age, sex, religion, economic status, residence, and so on. In contrast, psychographics refers to the "soft data": values, attitudes, beliefs, visions, and so on. It is important to analyze both areas about the reader.

Successful writers recognize the importance of understanding both demographic and psychographic information in order to meet the needs of the audience. For example, if I am a NASA scientist, and I am writing an article on a specific experiment, I need to know who will read my article. Will it be read by other experts, by community citizens, or by a third grade class? Audience analysis is going to play a key role in my approach as a writer. In fact, my entire approach will depend upon my audience's ability to understand.

Use the questions in Figure 9 or similar questions about your audience to help you focus your material and to achieve your goal to communicate effectively with your reader. The time you spend preparing your message based on reader's needs will be well spent.

Sample Letter Exchange Between Employee and Customer

In Figure 10, I have provided an exchange of letters between an employee and a customer. Read the exchange carefully and ask yourself why the employee responded as he or she did.

Figure 10: Letter Exchange

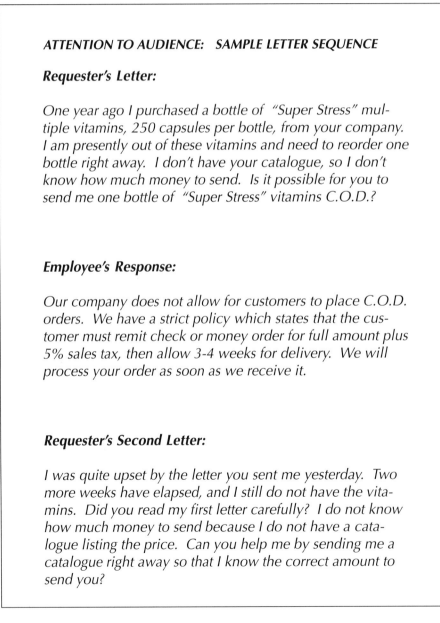

ATTENTION TO AUDIENCE: SAMPLE LETTER SEQUENCE

Requester's Letter:

One year ago I purchased a bottle of "Super Stress" multiple vitamins, 250 capsules per bottle, from your company. I am presently out of these vitamins and need to reorder one bottle right away. I don't have your catalogue, so I don't know how much money to send. Is it possible for you to send me one bottle of "Super Stress" vitamins C.O.D.?

Employee's Response:

Our company does not allow for customers to place C.O.D. orders. We have a strict policy which states that the customer must remit check or money order for full amount plus 5% sales tax, then allow 3-4 weeks for delivery. We will process your order as soon as we receive it.

Requester's Second Letter:

I was quite upset by the letter you sent me yesterday. Two more weeks have elapsed, and I still do not have the vitamins. Did you read my first letter carefully? I do not know how much money to send because I do not have a catalogue listing the price. Can you help me by sending me a catalogue right away so that I know the correct amount to send you?

In Figure 10, the requester's first letter was quite straightforward. The request was clear. The customer had specific needs that were not addressed or met in this exchange because the employee did not listen to the request. Of course, frustration resulted.

Why did the employee respond without listening carefully to the request? Unfortunately, all too often, people will respond to others, especially to customers, based on the "rules and regulations." The employee heard only the question being asked by the requester at the end of the letter regarding sending the vitamins C.O.D. That question was clearly not the full request.

As an effective business communicator, listen to the entire request to meet the customer's needs. By asking the questions listed below while prewriting, the employee could have responded fully to the customer's request.

Who is my reader?

*What does my reader **want**?*

*What does my reader **need**?*

*What does my reader **have** or **know** ALREADY?*

*What part of the request **can** be met?*

What extra actions not requested could be taken to show exceptional customer service?

Writing Exercises

(To practice skills in analyzing your audience, you may attempt the exercise found in Appendix C.)

CHAPTER 4

Evaluate Your Tone

Tone refers to the "attitude" that the writer expresses in the written message. Just as we are affected by the feelings presented to us by a person's attitude, every writer projects a certain attitude that impacts the reader. This is true whether you are writing a memo, a letter, an essay, a report, or any other type of document. That attitude may range from formal, traditional, and acceptable, to obnoxious and dictatorial. Look at the following samples and decide what you think the writer's attitude is in Sample 1. Compare the change in tone in Sample 2.

Sample 1:

Where is the information you were supposed to send me? Get it to me immediately. You're holding me up. You know I can't prepare our annual report without it.

Sample 2:

Please send me the requested information by Friday morning so that I can prepare our annual report. I am concerned about being able to meet the deadline. If this presents a problem for you, please call me immediately (283-0001) so that we can discuss it. Thanks.

Notice that the words chosen create the tone of the message. In Sample 1, words like "supposed to," "immediately," "You're holding me up," "You know," create a blaming tone. It's clear that the writer is frustrated about not having received the necessary information. Perhaps, the writer is justified in feeling angry and frustrated. To be effective, however, the tone of the business writing needs to be factual and cooperative at all costs. The goal of the writer is to create shared meaning that will not be received defensively. Thinking of only his or her own situation is counterproductive for the writer who wishes to communicate effectively.

In Sample 2, stating specifics such as "Friday morning" instead of "immediately" will also help to ensure that the writer gets what he or she wants while maintaining an assertive and respectful stance. Likewise, in this message the writer covers all bases by stating what is expected if the request cannot be met. The receiver of this message is obligated to take some action for the benefit of the writer without feeling insulted or attacked.

Essential Elements of Tone

When evaluating and creating your tone, consider the four primary elements reflected in an effective tone: **personal**, **natural**, **tactful**, and **positive**.

Personal Tone

Let's begin by evaluating how to create a personal tone. If you have considered your audience and your situation and have determined that a personal tone is your desire, you next need to select words that will help you to create that personal tone. Notice the sentence examples in Figure 11. The first sentence in each pair is considered to be more neutral in tone. The second is more personal. What creates the personal tone?

Notice that the more personal examples simply use personal word choices. Especially effective is the use of "you." The examples in Exercise 1 are real business examples. What can be done to create a more effective, personal tone? Try to revise the sentences first; then read the suggestions included in Appendix D to compare your attempt.

Figure 11: Creating a Personal Tone

1. *It is requested that this department receive your request for vacation early.*

   Sending us your vacation request early would ensure a timely response.

2. *There is an attachment included.*

   I'm including an attachment.

3. *It is essential that you comply with our request. We shall have to institute legal action against you if you do not remit the full amount of your liability by May 4.*

   If you send us your check by May 4, you'll avoid our taking legal action.

4. *We regret to inform you that the notebooks you ordered are not available. Because of this, we have been forced to cancel your order.*

   Since our recent offer was popular, we have run out of notebooks. Although we must cancel your order, we hope to have a similar promotion soon and will put your name at the top of our mailing list.

Exercise 4-1: Revise these sentences to improve the tone.

1. We note in your letter of July 14 that you claim not to have received your order. We will issue a second order to be sent without delay.

2. We were disappointed to learn you aren't taking advantage of our offer of a week's free advertising space. This was a favor we offered you at no benefit to us.

3. It is strongly suggested that you complete this project as soon as possible.

Using a Personal Point of View

Note the impact of using "YOU" in the following examples:

1. *Our employees' suggestions are always appreciated.*

 Your suggestions are always appreciated.

2. *Our customers are invited to stop in and see our newest stereos.*

 You're invited to stop in and see our newest stereos.

3. *A good evaluation can be a person's most important asset.*

 Your good evaluation can be your most important asset.

Stress the Reader's Benefits

If it is possible, stress the benefits to be gained by the reader.
If you are trying to persuade the reader, keep your needs secondary.

1. *To help <u>us</u> update <u>our</u> inventory and to keep you informed about the status of your order, please complete the enclosed form.*

 To keep <u>you</u> informed about the status of <u>your</u> order and to help us update our inventory, please complete the enclosed form.

2. *<u>Our</u> new floor covering is the best <u>we've</u> ever created because it will withstand great stress.*

 <u>You</u> can rely on <u>your</u> new floor covering to withstand great stress.

Exercise 4-2: Revise these sentences to improve the tone. Compare your attempt with the examples provided in Appendix D.

1. We would like to take this opportunity to thank you for attending our banquet.

2. I have received your request to take a vacation during the month of December.

3. Our new calculators are guaranteed for three years, so our customers can be sure they are getting a quality machine.

Natural Tone

In addition to striving for a personal tone in order to address the reader more directly, we also want to have a natural tone in our writing. I tell business people to "write like they would talk" providing their speech is not full of slang or language that is too informal.

Often in business, writers feel compelled to send memos with statements such as "Herewith noted is receipt of said document." My question to writers in my workshops is "Would you walk into a person's office, hand the person the document, and make that statement?" Almost always, participants laugh yet admit that they have written statements like that.

Work toward a more natural tone. You'll be surprised at how much easier writing becomes when you do not feel the need to twist it unnaturally.

Figure 12 provides writing samples that have been revised from an unnatural to a more natural tone.

Figure 12: Creating a Natural Tone

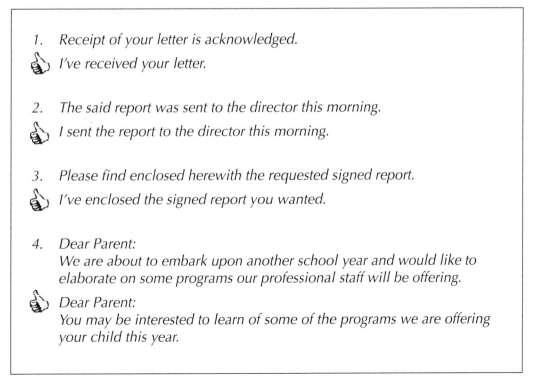

1. *Receipt of your letter is acknowledged.*
    I've received your letter.

2. *The said report was sent to the director this morning.*
    I sent the report to the director this morning.

3. *Please find enclosed herewith the requested signed report.*
    I've enclosed the signed report you wanted.

4. *Dear Parent:*
    We are about to embark upon another school year and would like to elaborate on some programs our professional staff will be offering.
    Dear Parent:
    You may be interested to learn of some of the programs we are offering your child this year.

Tired and Overused Expressions

Certain expressions are considered in business to be "tired" or "overused." To some extent they can create a tone that doesn't seem natural, honest, or authentic even though the tone is considered acceptable business jargon. Note that we are saying "acceptable," not "effective." Evaluate your own documents against the list in Figure 13.

Figure 13: Tired and Overused Expressions

> *I would like to take this opportunity*
>
> *For your convenience we have enclosed a self-addressed stamped envelope*
>
> *Thank you for your attention to this matter*
>
> *Pursuant to your telephone call*
>
> *Thanking you kindly in advance*
>
> *Your prompt response would be appreciated*
>
> *Attached please find; enclosed please find*
>
> *Our company policy dictates*
>
> *Kindly advise me as to your plans*
>
> *I remain yours truly*
>
> *Among those present*
>
> *Each and every one*
>
> *Every walk of life*
>
> *Goes without saying*
>
> *Acknowledge receipt of*
>
> *As per your request*
>
> *Enclosed herewith*

Can you think of more natural, creative ways to say the same thing? Let's look at the first two to get you started:

Statement 1: "I would like to take this opportunity." Why not just take it? Instead of "I would like to take this opportunity to congratulate you on your promotion," substitute "Congratulations on your promotion."

Statement 2 reads "For your convenience we have enclosed a self-addressed stamped envelope." Since the reader will know it is for his or her convenience, why not reword the statement: "We have enclosed a pre-paid envelope." Think of new ways to make routine statements less than routine-sounding. This is a partial list of tired and overused expressions. What others might you add?

Tactful Tone

It is often easier for writers to improve the personal and natural elements of tone in their writing than it is for them to improve the tactfulness of their message. Tactful messages require tactful senders. Notice the tactlessness of the following first examples in each pair in Figure 14 as contrasted with the more tactful second examples.

Figure 14: Creating a Tactful Tone

1. *The request that you sent for overtime pay is completely out of line because our policy makes it clear that you will not be paid overtime until after 40 hours.*

   Your request for overtime pay cannot be accepted because the policy is that overtime will be paid after 40 hours.

2. *It seems like you didn't understand our instructions. We specifically told you to grease the wheels once a month to prevent rust.*

   Our instructions were to grease the wheels once a month to prevent rust. Notice in your instruction manual, in paragraph 2 on page 3, important information on greasing the machinery. Please call us if you have questions.

Words and Phrases with Undesirable Overtones

It is important to be aware of certain words that create an undesirable tone. Figure 15 provides examples of such words. You may want to add examples of your own.

Figure 15: Words and Phrases with Undesirable Overtones

Apparently you are not aware
Our records show
We are not inclined to
We cannot understand your
We do not agree with your
We question your
We repeated to you
We hope you'll be prompt
Why didn't you
You apparently overlooked
You are accountable for
You are misinformed
You are wrong
You claim
You complain
You contend
You do not realize
You do not understand
You failed to
You forgot to
You led us to believe
You may be right but
You must realize
You neglected to
You overlooked
You state
You will have to
You delayed
You demanded
You don't make yourself clear
Since we usually know
We are right even though
You're responsible—We aren't
Your carelessness caused
We order you to
When you question our

Positive Tone

In most business situations we desire to have a positive or neutral tone. In certain situations such as in giving simple information about when a policy will be effective, you can choose to deliver the information in a "negative" or a "positive" way. For example, you can say "Your insurance will not be effective until October 2" (negative), or you can say, "Your insurance will be effective on October 2" (positive). Notice the following examples in Figure 16 that contrast the negative and positive tones.

Figure 16: Creating a Positive Tone

1. *It is against our policy to allow you to hold more than one job.*

   It is our policy to allow you to hold only one job.

2. *We regret to tell you that your washing machine will not be repaired until Wednesday.*

   Your washing machine will be repaired on Wednesday. We are sorry for any inconvenience.

3. *We have received the said letter about the alleged loss of your computer.*

   Your letter of December 10 about the loss of your computer has been received.

4. *We cannot process your order the same day that we receive it due to our limited number of staff members.*

   Your order is important to us and will be processed within two days of its receipt. By employing a two-member staff, we are able to keep your prices low and give each order individualized attention. Please don't hesitate to call if you should have questions.

Exercise 4-3: Evaluate and revise each of the following examples to improve the tone. Check your answers against those listed for this exercise in Appendix D.

1. Herewith noted is receipt of said payment.

2. On each of the monthly statements our firm sends to its customers, it is indicated that payment must be made within ten days.

3. It sounds as if you didn't follow the instructions in the operator's manual about oiling the mechanism.

4. If you don't reply immediately, we won't be able to ship your equipment.

5. Reference is made to your letter of April 17 about our weekly meeting.

6. I thought I made it perfectly clear the last time we talked. No, I am not attending the meeting.

7. If the interviewee doesn't arrive on time for her appointment, she won't be treated with as much consideration.

8. The group report will probably be late because of Ed's inefficient use of time. He caused everyone else to have less time to get their portions finished.

Summary

In summary, when your writing conveys an effective tone or "attitude," the chance of your message being received favorably by the reader is greater. Above all, remember that the tone of your message impacts your business reputation.

CHAPTER 5

Create an Effective Style

In Chapter 4, we referred to **tone** as the "attitude" that a certain piece of writing projects. In comparison, **style** might refer to the "appearance" that the writing carries. For example, is the style "wordy," "abrupt," "succinct," or "flowery"? These are some words that people use to describe writers' styles. Take a look at the following three styles for comparison of effectiveness.

Sample 1: Wordy Style

It is strongly suggested that the entire staff, this being the inclusion of all levels of employees in grades 8-13, be in attendance at the "Managing Change" workshop to be held on Friday, April 1, at 4:00 p.m. in the afternoon in Training Room B located in Hoffler Hall. Please be aware that all such employees are encouraged to attend and to participate in this worthwhile program no matter what their classification status. With the extensive restructuring we are endeavoring to embark upon next month, this program has the prospect of providing some highly advantageous and beneficial information to guide us through a potentially perilous time.

Sample 2: Abrupt Style

On Friday, April 1, at 4:00 p.m., there's a meeting in Training Room B on "Managing Change." You are required to attend.

Sample 3: Effective Style

Please plan to attend a workshop on Friday, April 1, at 4:00 p.m. in Hoffler Hall, Training Room B. The program, "Managing Change," comes highly recommended by the American Leadership Association. Given the restructuring that we are facing next month, I think this program will provide some useful information. If you have a schedule conflict, please let me know. Thanks.

Critique of Samples

Notice that Sample 3 provides complete information about the specifics of the workshop yet also encourages the employee to attend by providing a reason why. Still, the memo itself is relatively concise and to the point.

Remember that in business, time is money. Few people want to read a two-page memo when a one-page memo will do. In addition, if you are writing lengthy sentences, certain readers simply will not understand you.

It may be helpful to know how the readability of a piece of writing is calculated. Generally, the length of the sentence (the number of words in the sentence) and the number of syllables in the words (for example, "compensation" has four syllables—"com-pen-sa-tion" versus "pay" which has one syllable) create the readability level. Therefore, if your sentences are longer and you use high-level generalized or specialized words, your writing will require that a person be able to read at a higher level.

Wordiness

Let's look at a chart of phrases that can create wordiness (Figure 17). Evaluate your own writing against this chart. The phrases on the left can be replaced by briefer choices on the right. Below I have added phrases that provide what could be called "unnecessary qualification." In other words, if something is "round in shape," could it be "round" in anything else?

Figure 18 is a chart of additional wordy expressions. Both charts can be used as tools to evaluate your own writing style.

Avoid Unnecessary Qualification:

round **in shape**
many **in number**
blue **in color**
during **the year of** 1995
for **a price of** $200
longer **in length**
larger **in size**
in **the city of** Chicago
second time **in my life**
honest **in character**
quickly **with haste**
audible **to the ear**
tasted bitter **to the tongue**

Figure 17: Eliminating Wordiness

Instead of:	*Try:*
due to the fact that	because
in order to	to
for the purposes of	to or so
in the event that	if
in such a manner or way so as to	so
in an effort to	to
by means of	with
in connection with	with
for the length of time that	while
with the result that	so
is supportive of	supports
to be of great benefit	benefits
in such a state that	so or such
pertains to the problem of	concerns
at this point in time	now
am (or are) in agreement with	agree
to make an effort to	to
insofar as	so
with reference to	regarding
in spite of the fact that	in spite of or despite
a large number of	many, several
at a later date	later
in the near future	soon
my personal opinion	my opinion
your letter under date of	your letter of
in view of the fact that	since, because
sometime in the early part of next month	early next month
in a satisfactory manner	satisfactorily
we are of the opinion that	we believe
enclosed herewith is.	I've enclosed
for the reason that	because

Figure 18: Additional Wordy Expressions

Instead of: .... *Try:*

absolutely complete..................................complete
anticipate ahead......................................anticipate
anxious and eager....................................anxious or eager
as of this date...yet, still, or now
as yet..still
ascent up to..ascent
ask the question......................................ask
assemble together at 4 p.m. in the afternoon...assemble at 4 p.m.
basic fundamentals...................................fundamentals
carbon copy of..copy
combined together with............................combined with
concluded at the end................................concluded
consensus of opinion...............................consensus or opinion
continue on..continue
cooperate together...................................cooperate
cost and expense......................................cost or expense
demand and insist....................................demand or insist
due to the fact...due to, since, because
each and every..each or every
entirely complete......................................entirely or complete
evident and apparent.................................evident or apparent
exactly the same......................................same
fall down..fall
first began to...began
first and foremost.....................................first
for the period of a month...........................or a month
full and complete......................................full or complete
important essentials..................................essentials
in any way, shape, or form.........................in any way
initial beginning.......................................beginning
refer back to..refer to
right and proper.......................................right or proper
rise up...rise
same identical...same
still continue..continue
true facts..truth or facts
You owe a total of $215............................You owe $215.

Style: Use Specific Words

In addition to improving the document style by reducing the wordiness, using specific words rather than vague words will also improve the style and increase the chance for shared meaning between sender and receiver. In Figure 19 notice the first sentence in each pair. It carries a vague meaning as compared to the more specific second example. What is your goal with your reader? Do you want to be sure that the reader understands? Use specific words to convey specific meaning.

Figure 19: Using Specific Words

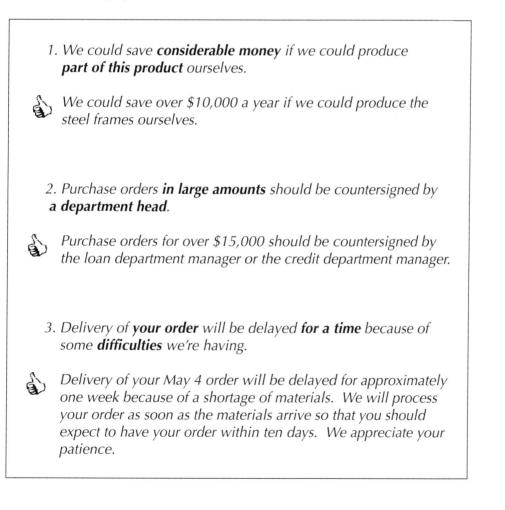

1. *We could save **considerable money** if we could produce **part of this product** ourselves.*

   We could save over $10,000 a year if we could produce the steel frames ourselves.

2. *Purchase orders **in large amounts** should be countersigned by **a department head**.*

   Purchase orders for over $15,000 should be countersigned by the loan department manager or the credit department manager.

3. *Delivery of **your order** will be delayed **for a time** because of some **difficulties** we're having.*

   Delivery of your May 4 order will be delayed for approximately one week because of a shortage of materials. We will process your order as soon as the materials arrive so that you should expect to have your order within ten days. We appreciate your patience.

Watch Ambiguous Wording

Effective communication also depends upon completing the meaning in our statements so that the reader understands us fully. If we write with an ambiguous meaning, our reader will not know specifically what we are saying. Look at the sentences in Figure 20. Decide what each sentence could mean.

Figure 20: Watching Ambiguous Wording

---

1.   *I don't know Elvira **as well as** Monique.*

2.   *This modern chair will **eliminate** tired patients.*

3.   *Mr. Shirley **tried very hard to get along with** his co-workers.*

Sentence 1 in Figure 20 carries several meanings: "I don't know Elvira *as well as I know Monique,*" "I don't know Elvira *as well as Monique knows Elvira,*" or "I don't know *Elvira OR Monique.*"

The writer of sentence 2 probably intends for the chair to cushion or soothe the patient so that the feeling of tiredness is eliminated. Instead, the writer has eliminated the patient.

Sentence 3 is ambiguous since we are not sure whether the statement is intended to compliment Mr. Shirley or to state that Mr. Shirley was unsuccessful in his attempts. What does it mean to say he "tried very hard to get along"? Did he succeed? Did he not? If this statement were written as a part of Mr. Shirley's evaluation for his work performance, it would be critical that the statement reflect clearly what the writer thought of Mr. Shirley's performance.

Recognize Specialized Jargon

Technical jargon serves as a shortcut and is fine to use if you're writing to people within your technical group. Every business area has certain technical terms and acronyms that are used for convenience and to provide full expression. The problem occurs when specialized terms are not defined for certain audience levels. If your client, customer, or co-worker may not know your jargon, define it. *Consider your reader at all times.*

Avoid Inflated Words

In addition to watching specialized jargon, consider the impact of inflated words on the reader's ability to comprehend the message. Inflated words might alienate your reader depending upon his or her ability. See Figure 21 for examples.

Figure 21: Watching Inflated Words

---

1.   This incombustible material will reduce the dissemination of flames.

     This fireproof material will reduce the spread of flames.

2.   I'll endeavor to ascertain whether the date of the shipment is subject to modification.

     I'll try to find out whether the shipment date can be changed.

In Figure 21, the first sentence in each pair includes words that would be difficult for the average person to comprehend. If a word in a sentence is unclear or if more than one word is unclear, a person would use the other words to determine the meaning within the context. If too many words are unclear, meaning is lost.

Is there an advantage to writing in a style that uses inflated words? Some may argue that if you know your reader well and believe that the reader appreciates higher-level language using such a style is preferable. For general audiences, however, in which the reader is unknown, it is almost always problematic to inflate your language.

When a writer insists on using high-level generalized vocabulary no matter what the reader's needs, I suggest that the writer look closely at his or her motive. Some individuals hold on to the same hairstyle or chosen dress for every occasion. The person who uses inflated words in all writing situations is like a person who insists on wearing a tuxedo at all times, even to the beach.

Remember that the goal of effective business communication is shared meaning. Analyze the reader's ability to understand your words. Figure 22 provides a list of inflated and simplified words for comparison.

Figure 22: Chart of Inflated Words

Inflated Vocabulary	Simpler Vocabulary
ascertain	find out
compensation	pay
conglomeration	mixture
contiguous	near
disseminate	spread
elucidate	clarify
endeavor	try
noncombustible	fireproof
innocuous	harmless
modification	change
obviate	prevent
orifice	opening
quadrilateral	four-sided
ramification	consequence
transmit	send
vacillate	waver
veracious	true

Pay Attention to Sentence Structure

Certain word processing computer programs assist writers with grammar information. Workshop participants have often asked me to help them decipher the information that they have received in these programs. For example, some people have said, "I've been told by the program that I have passive voice. Is it okay to have passive voice? What's wrong with passive voice?"

Quite simply, knowing that you have used passive voice in a sentence does not necessarily mean that your sentence is less effective. In fact, passive voice may be the preferred form for your situation.

So, what is passive voice and active voice? Look at the following sentences.

Passive Voice: *The letter was written by Damian.*

Active Voice: *Damian wrote the letter.*

In the passive voice sentence, the subject is "letter" and the verb is "was written." To say that the sentence is passive voice is simply to indicate that the subject is receiving the action of the verb. The letter is not doing anything; it is receiving the action. In the active voice sentence, "Damian" is the subject and "wrote" is the verb. Since Damian is doing the writing or the verb action, we say that the verb is in active voice.

As a writer, you need to decide in your situation whether passive or active voice would prove more to your advantage in delivering your message. What follows are some advantages and disadvantages of passive voice:

Passive voice
   . . .can create variety and can be used to place the reader first.
   . . .can emphasize the receiver of the action rather than the performer.
   . . .can be used effectively to create formal report style.

Passive voice
   . . .can produce wordiness and awkward phrasing.
   . . .can fail to say who is performing the action.
   . . .can slow the reader down.

Exercise 5-1: Revise the following passive voice constructions in each sentence into active voice. Check your answers for this exercise against those listed in Appendix D.

Example of Passive Voice Revised:

The research project will be supervised by Professor Bruce.
Professor Bruce will supervise the research project.

Exercise 5-1: Change the following passive constructions into active ones.

1. *The memo was sent by Marcia Moore three weeks ago.*

2. *The check was awarded to the hospital by our assistant manager.*

3. *The child was bitten on her left arm by a stray dog.*

4. *Matthew was given the Science Merit award for his division by his teacher.*

5. *The new couple was sent a "welcome basket" by their neighbors on Main Street.*

Structure: Sentence Formation Impacts Meaning

How we create or form our sentences—what words we place before others—is important. In your academic writing classes, you may recall being told that you had a **dangling modifier** or a **misplaced element**. For many of us, we remember the images of "disease" that the terms brought up. Understanding problematic structures and how to revise them doesn't have to be painful. In fact, with knowledge and awareness, you can eliminate problematic structures with ease. Look at the following sentence and decide on its meaning:

Swimming in my soup, I saw a fly.

Were you swimming in your soup or was the fly swimming? To correct the sentence, write:

I saw a fly swimming in my soup.

Notice the examples in Figure 23 of dangling sentence parts (dangling modifiers), misplaced elements, and questions of sentence logic. In parentheses after each first sentence, I have asked you a question and made comments to help you to see what the faulty construction may be implying.

Figure 23: Problematic Structures

Dangling Sentence Parts:

1. While visiting your Norfolk branch, a number of problems were discovered.

(Did the number of problems visit the Norfolk branch? Notice that the phrase "While visiting your Norfolk branch" does not attach itself effectively to the main subject in the sentence "a number." In order to connect the phrase to what it actually modifies, you will need to reword the sentence as indicated below.)

While visiting your Norfolk branch, the security team discovered a number of problems.

2. As an agent for the Metro Insurance Company, payment of your claim can be authorized by me.

(The way that the sentence is structured, the implication is that the payment is the agent. Remember that the first phrase in the sentence "As an agent for Metro Insurance Company" needs to be connected to what it modifies. Who is the agent? In this case, of course, the agent is "I," the writer.)

As an agent for the Metro Insurance Company, I can authorize payment of your claim.

(Notice that in this revised sentence, the word "I" is next to the phrase that modifies it.)

Misplaced Elements:

1. During the dark of the night, the camper shot a bear in his pajamas.

(Was the bear wearing the pajamas? In this example, "in his pajamas" is placed next to the noun "a bear" implying that the bear is wearing the pajamas. Place the descriptive phrase next to what it actually modifies.)

 During the dark of the night while still in his pajamas, the camper shot a bear.

2. This pre-employment package contains our standard application form and an employee's handbook that you should fill out and return.

(Should you fill out and return the handbook? Believe me, someone will attempt to fill out and return the handbook if you word your sentence in this way.)

 This pre-employment package contains an employee's handbook and our standard application form that you should fill out and return.

Sentence Logic:

1. As soon as they are corrected, these errors will improve our profit report.

(How can errors improve a report? In addition to having dangling modifiers and misplaced elements, sometimes if we simply look at the logic of our words, we would know that a sentence's meaning is impossible.)

 Correcting these errors will improve our profit report.

2. This accounting method took as long as five days to implement the program.

(How can a method implement a program?)

 Using this accounting method, we implemented the program in five days.

(Being aware of the importance of word order and the interactions of words will help you to say what you want to say more clearly.)

Exercise 5-2: Read each sentence and revise any dangling modifiers, misplaced elements, or illogical constructions. Check your answers against suggestions provided in Appendix D.

1. Opened last year, Kamil frequently uses his charge account.

2. Anticipating her response, the report annoyed Beatrice as she read it.

3. Parking is permitted in the lot by the attendant that is identified with the blue marker.

4. As a new employee, managers provide training sessions to orient you.

5. He ordered five dozen markers for his committee members with pocket clips on them.

Use Lists to Communicate Clearly

Another simple structure to order information effectively is the device of using lists. Using a list can work to your advantage to break up heavy textual information as well as to give the reader a visual break. Figure 24 provides simple rules for using lists effectively.

Figure 24: Use Lists to Communicate Clearly

The Advantages of Using Lists

To write more effectively, use lists when possible to:

- make writing easier since lists organize material naturally

- make reading faster since lists are visually easier to follow

- reduce error possibilities since grammar and mechanics are simplified.

Simple Rules for Using Lists

1. Introduce a list with a statement.

To introduce you to our products, we are offering you the following:

- a 15% discount on your initial purchase

- a one-month trial period to test the product

- a special gift awarded when you register for credit.

2. Use neutral symbols to mark items in your list. Use numbers only to indicate priority or steps in a series.

<u>AVOID</u> We are interested in the following:
(A.) ——————————
(B.) ——————————
(C.) ——————————
or
* ————————————
* ————————————

(Asterisks can confuse readers who expect traditional use.)

<u>USE</u> We are interested in the following:
- ——————————
- ——————————
- ——————————.

If you do choose to number items in a series of steps, avoid unnecessary parentheses such as in the following examples:

    1)   or   1.)   or   (1)

(See conventional list numbering in number 3. It is less cluttered looking.)

3. Use punctuation at the end of the line only when at least one item has internal commas or when the items are sentences.

Sample 1: No punctuation is needed in this series:

Shamika was interested in the following majors:
- Chemistry
- Mathematics
- Engineering
- English. (*Notice that a period is placed after "English" since the entire piece is a sentence.*)

Sample 2: Punctuation is needed since at least one item has internal commas:

The menu provided three "specials":
1. Ham with sweet potatoes, corn, and biscuits;
2. Turkey with dressing, green beans, and yams;
3. Chicken with mashed potatoes, dumplings, and applesauce.

(In this example, using the numbers 1,2,3 might be helpful for the customer to indicate a preference more easily as in "I'll have special number 1.")

Sample 3: Punctuation is needed since each item is a sentence. Periods are appropriate on each line.

Follow these steps to ensure safety when closing the shop:
1. Turn on the inside night lights and all outside security lights.
2. Lock all outside access doors.
3. Turn off all electrical equipment.
4. Turn on the answering machine.

4. Keep items in the list parallel. (Present items in the same form.)

AVOID Our new marketing strategy includes:
- offering a 15% discount to new buyers
- a complimentary gift to credit applicants
- previewing the 1997 models.

USE Our new marketing strategy includes:
- a 15% discount offer to new buyers
- a complimentary gift to credit applicants
- a preview of the 1997 models.

Using a list effectively can greatly enhance the reader's ability to receive the information with ease. In letters, memos, reports, proposals—and especially in e-mail—using lists can simplify the information so that the reader can quickly grasp it. A list provides a visual advantage to the standard paragraph.

CHAPTER 6

Writing Effective Letters

The most frequently written business documents are letters and memos. Letters are written to convey your message to someone outside your organization while memos are usually written to convey information inside your organization. To some extent, e-mail (electronic mail) has bridged the gap between letters and memos since it can be used to send information both inside and outside your organization. E-mail has become as popular, if not more popular, in the workplace than written, hard-copy memos.

Whatever the medium of your message, **the key to successful business writing is to recognize that it involves planning and adapting the material to a specific format, or order.** This chapter will provide information on the general types of letters we write most frequently in business and on how to approach the formatting of those letters.

Letter Writing

While you may find hundreds of different situations that require you to write a letter, the news that you convey in a letter falls into one of three general categories based on how the news will be received:

- **favorable news** (news that is positive or neutral)
- **negative news** (news that will probably be received unfavorably)
- **persuasive news** (news that persuades the reader to listen and to take action).

Understanding the format of these three general plans can save you valuable time in preparing your message. Figure 25 provides information on these three formats. Take a look at these three types before we look more closely at the favorable news plan.

Figure 25: Three Basic Formats for Letters

FAVORABLE NEWS PLAN:
USE THE FAVORABLE PLAN
TO DELIVER POSITIVE OR NEUTRAL NEWS.

Format:
1. *Deliver the Main News.*
2. *Add Necessary Details.*
3. *Close Positively.*

NEGATIVE NEWS PLAN:
USE THE NEGATIVE PLAN
TO DELIVER NEGATIVE NEWS.

Format:
1. *Open with a Buffer Statement.*
2. *Start Giving Reasons for Refusing.*
3. *Refuse. (Make Refusal Clear.)*
4. *Give More Reasons for Refusing. If Possible, Offer an Alternative.*
5. *Close on a Positive Note if Possible.*

PERSUASIVE NEWS PLAN:
USE THE PERSUASIVE PLAN TO CONVINCE THE READER TO TAKE ACTION OR TO CHOOSE A SPECIFIC OPTION.

Format:
1. *Open with an Attention-Getting Statement.*
2. *Interest the Reader in the Subject.*
3. *Build the Reader's Desire to Act.*
4. *Close with the Action Request.*

The Favorable News Plan

The majority of business letters are written under the favorable news plan. The purpose of this format is to convey information that will be taken positively or at least taken from a neutral standpoint. A favorable news letter might involve asking or granting a routine request or simply providing routine information.

These letters may also be written to promote "goodwill" – to congratulate or to thank someone for a service. Unfortunately, letters that could be written to promote goodwill often are not written. Too frequently, people write only when they want or need something. If you have favorable news that could in any way build goodwill between you and another person, by all means write the letter. While you may not be meeting what seems like an immediate goal, in the long term you will be promoting effective public relations between you and a client, partner, boss, and so on.

In writing any favorable letter, you are able to start the letter with the main news since the news will be received favorably. In other words, start with the "congratulations," "thank you," or other favorable response or request. After providing the initial news, you may then proceed with the secondary details. End by closing positively.

Let's take a look at a letter that was NOT written using the favorable news plan; then look at how it may have been written from a favorable news plan approach. After reading these two letters and comparing the formats, read the critique that follows Figure 26. (These letters do not include the full typing format for letters. If you desire more information on typing styles, refer to Appendix B.)

Figure 26: The Favorable News Plan: Sample Letter Set 1 for a Routine Request

---

Letter 1: *NOT* Using the Favorable News Plan

Dear Sir,

I was impressed with your article in <u>Pilot</u> magazine regarding what seems like a fool-proof procedure for writing a report. I have to write numerous reports on the job so your book interests me.

I'd like to receive a copy of your book as advertised. Your article doesn't indicate how long to allow for shipping and time. I trust that you will send me as promptly as possible a copy of this book. I have enclosed a check to cover cost and shipping.

Sincerely,

Figure 26: (Continued)

Letter 2:   USING the Favorable News Plan

Dear Sir/Madam:

Please send me a copy of your book A Fool-Proof Procedure for Report Writing. I have enclosed a check for $31.25 to cover cost and shipping.

I was impressed with your article in Pilot and because I must write reports frequently on the job, I look forward to receiving your book as soon as possible. Thank you.

Sincerely,

Critique of Sample Letter Set 1: A Routine Request

Letter 1

Notice that Letter 1 begins with "Dear Sir." In a business letter, unless we are sure that the recipient is male, we should use the more standard term "Dear Sir/Madam" or "Dear Madam/Sir" in order not to make a sexist assumption. Additionally, the salutation should be followed by a colon [:] and not by a comma in a standard business letter. Reserve commas for use in personal letters.

Notice also that Letter 1 begins with secondary information. The main news is the request for the book. By beginning with secondary news first, the writer of Letter 1 has put the reader at a disadvantage for identifying the main point of the letter.

The tone of Letter 1 is likewise not very effective. Statements like "I trust you will send me as promptly as possible" lend an air of arrogance that is simply not helpful. No specifics are given either: title of book, amount of check, and so on.

Letter 2

In Letter 2, the main news is identified in the first sentence: the request for a specific book. It is followed by the statement that the check is enclosed for a specific amount. The second paragraph provides secondary information that may or may not be necessary to convey to this reader; however, the writer adds it to provide an appropriate closing for a favorable letter and to establish a good reader/writer relationship.

Here is a second sample of two letters, one not using the favorable news plan and one using the favorable news plan.

Figure 27: The Favorable News Plan:
Sample Letter Set 2 for Sending Goodwill

Letter 1: <u>NOT</u> Using the Favorable Plan

Dear Mr. Brooks:

I was looking in the Virginian Daily Press *yesterday and noticed that you had been promoted to Manager of Micrographics Industry. I wanted to tell you how happy I am for you that you have achieved a well deserved promotion. I used to work in the design department at Graphics Trade so I'm not sure whether you remember me when you worked there.*

I wish you the very best in your future endeavors, especially as manager.

All the Best,

Letter 2: <u>USING</u> the Favorable Plan

Dear Mr. Brooks:

Congratulations on your promotion to Manager of Micrographics Industry. Having worked in the design department at Graphics Trade when you were manager of productions there, I recall how well you handled deadlines and the enthusiasm you had for challenging projects. I'm so happy that you've achieved this well deserved promotion.

I wish you the very best in your new position.

Sincerely,

Critique of Sample Letter Set 2: The Goodwill Message

Letter 1

The first letter does not follow the favorable news format since it does not start with the main news. Instead, secondary information is provided about the writer and where she saw the news. Even her relationship to the receiver is tentatively stated. While the tone is appropriate and friendly, the message is weak in its delivery. Also the last line wishes the receiver "the best of luck" and the closing of "all the best" seems redundant.

Letter 2

The second letter begins with the main news of "congratulations" at the forefront. Immediately, the writer ties in her relationship to the receiver in terms of how she viewed him from their previous work together. The tone is upbeat and positive, and the message is provided in descending order of importance—in deductive style as described in Figure 25.

Negative News Plan

A negative news letter may be the most difficult letter to write. Who wants to learn that he or she didn't get the job or that a request for action must be refused? As a writer who delivers negative news, you must very carefully consider your reader. It may be helpful to review Chapter 3 on Audience. In the negative news letter format, you must consider the psychographics and demographics of your audience very carefully. What will the reader's attitude be toward receiving your negative news message? How are you able to deliver the negative message with less negative impact?

Let's look at a set of negative news letters presented in Figure 28. The first letter delivers the negative news but not according to the negative news plan described in Figure 25. The second letter uses the negative news plan described in Figure 25. A critique of the letters will follow.

Figure 28: The Negative News Plan:
Sample Letter Set 1 for Sending Negative News

Letter 1:   *NOT Using the Negative News Plan*

Dear Ms. Willowby:

I regret that I will be unable to present at your secretary association's big meeting in June. I do appreciate your asking me to be the guest speaker.

As you know, I have had a great deal of secretarial experience during my four years at Murphy's and also after that at Sampson's. Therefore, I do feel that I understand the secretary's needs.

Unfortunately, though, I will be delivering a presentation in the city of Chicago at a national meeting. If I can think of anyone who might be able to do your talk, I will let you know.

Of course, if you should need me to speak again, please let me know. Hopefully, it will work out in the future.

Sincerely,

Figure 28: (Continued)

Letter 2:   _USING_ the Negative News Plan

Dear Ms. Willowby:

The Legal Association of Secretaries is a prestigious organization, and I appreciate the invitation to speak at your May meeting.

On May 25, the day of your program, I will be in Chicago, presenting at another national meeting. Janice Jones, our district manager, is an excellent speaker, however, and has presented to various organizations on the topic of writing and the legal secretary. She has told me that she would be happy to speak for your group. She can be reached at 804-235-1234.

If you should again need support for your programs, please feel free to call or to write me. I will be glad to do whatever I can to assist you.

Sincerely,

Critique of Sample Letter Set 1: The Negative News Message

Letter 1

Letter 1 opens with the negative news "I regret." It is best in a negative news letter to keep the negative news out of the opening. Paragraph two simply tells the reader what the reader probably already knows. Why else would the reader have asked the presenter to do the speech?

In addition, the tone of this letter sounds pompous due to specific word choices: The writer will be "delivering a presentation in the city of Chicago" and mentions that if he can "think of anyone who might be able *to do your talk*" he'll let the reader know.   Likewise, in an effective negative news letter, the writer will offer an alternative if that is possible. (See the Negative News Plan outlined in Figure 25.) In Letter 1 in Figure 28, the alternative mentioned is not helpful and doesn't sound sincere.

Letter 2

Letter 2 delivers the negative news but without sounding overly negative. The writer is unable to accommodate the reader, makes that clear, yet opens with a buffer statement and provides a helpful alternative. The focus in Letter 2 is on the reader, not the writer.

In delivering negative news, remember to sound supportive if at all possible. Let the reader know that you have carefully considered the situation and that you care about the reader's interests even though the information you must send will probably be received negatively. Explaining your reasons for refusing will be necessary if the reason is not obvious. In this example, the writer clearly cannot be in two places at once, so the reason is clear.

Using passive voice may be effective in delivering negative news. (See passive voice in Chapter 5.) Often passive voice can soften the statement and take the attention off the reader as the recipient. For example, saying "You cannot receive what you have requested" focuses on the reader, the "you." "The request must be denied" puts the focus on the request.

Figure 29: The Negative News Plan:
Sample Letter Set 2 for Sending Negative News

Letter 1: <u>NOT</u> Using the Negative Plan

Dear Mr. Overstreet:

We are sorry to inform you that you did not receive the secretarial position for which you applied on March 10 with Hopewell Manor.

We wish you the best in your future job searches.

Sincerely,

Letter 2: <u>USING</u> the Negative Plan

Dear Mr. Overstreet:

The Hopewell Manor Search Committee met on March 12 and carefully reviewed over 30 applications received for the position of secretary.

While you were not chosen for the current position, we appreciate your taking the time to apply. Your application will be kept on file for consideration should future positions open.

Thank you.

Sincerely,

Critique of Sample Letter Set 2: The Negative News Message

Letter 1

The first letter is certainly concise and gets to the point immediately. In most business situations, this would be admirable. When delivering negative news, however, the conciseness comes across as abruptness, and the immediate delivery of the main message is too harsh for the reader. Even though the letter closes with a fairly decent tone, the overall feeling that the reader receives is heavy and negative.

Letter 2

To soften the tone, Letter 2 does not begin with the negative message. In Figure 25 you recall that the negative news plan requires that you keep the negative news out of the opening. (See Figure 25 for delivering negative news.)   The second letter in this set opens with an effective buffer statement: "The Hopewell Manor Search Committee met . . . ." In addition, this statement lets the reader know that 30 people applied for the position. When the reader learns that he did not get the position, the news will be slightly easier to handle knowing that 28 other people also did not get the position.

The letter continues by letting the reader know that his application will be kept on file should future positions arise. In this situation, that is the best alternative that can be provided given the circumstances.

The Persuasive News Plan

Persuasion is an art. In most persuasive business situations, persuasion is used to move another person by his or her own will to some agreement or course of action. Knowing how to write effective persuasive documents is important since business often involves selling and asking others to take action.

Above all, effective persuaders know the individuals whom they are trying to persuade. They analyze the demographics and psychographics carefully (discussed in Chapter 3) and try to imagine the situation from the other person's viewpoint in order to know how to strategize.

When you must persuade someone through a letter, remember to prewrite carefully. Decide specifically what action you want to take place and think of the approach that will best suit that reader.

Take a look at the set of persuasive letters in Figure 30. Read each letter carefully, analyzing its effectiveness; then note the critique that follows.

Figure 30: The Persuasive News Plan: Sample Letter Set 1 for Persuading Your Reader

---

Letter 1: <u>NOT</u> Using the Persuasive Plan

Dear Parent:

We are conducting a survey across the country pertaining to computer use among school children aged 6-13. The objective of the research is to find out the extent of usage of computers by these children and the availability of the computers for usage.

Your name has been selected at random from a group of individuals who have children these ages. Your initial outlay will be to take only a few minutes to complete the enclosed questionnaire. Your answers will be held strictly confidential. No researcher will call you as a result of your sharing this information.

Please complete the enclosed questionnaire and return it to me as soon as possible. I have enclosed a self-addressed, stamped envelope for your convenience.

Sincerely,

Critique of Sample Letter Set 1: The Persuasive News Message

Letter 1

Letter 1 is factual. The reader will be informed about what the writer desires. The question, however, is whether or not the reader will be moved to take action based on the letter.

Persuasive letters do provide information but do not *just* provide information. Persuasive letters encourage, convince, sway the reader to listen, to care, and to take action.

Letter 2

Letter 2 personalizes its message for the reader by allowing that reader to make a difference. The writer invites each reader to take a specific action that may impact the individual reader and his or her children.

The writer has opened the letter by making a personal statement to get the reader's attention, has continued to build the reader's interest and desire, and has ended with an action request that is clear and direct. The writer displays a confident tone that the reader will desire to take the action.

In general, when writing persuasive letters, you can assist the reader to act by providing telephone numbers (in the letter or on the letterhead) or by enclosing business-reply cards, envelopes, or coupons. Do what you can to make the action as easy as possible. Try to ensure a "follow through" of the action request.

Remain positive with your information, be as cooperative and helpful as possible, and keep the letter as brief as possible. Nothing is worse than receiving a two- or three-page letter requesting a donation or action. In general, people are busy, and time is money. *Each word in the persuasive letter, more than in any other type of letter, should be necessary.* Above all, keep the reader's interest and desire in mind.

Letter 2: *USING* *the Persuasive Plan*

Dear Parent:

You can help make it possible for children at Margaret Elementary School to use a new computer. How?

By supplying us information about your children between the ages of 6 and 13 and their use of computers, your name will automatically be placed in a drawing to award a Zenith Personal Computer to Margaret Elementary School.

How can you supply that information? We have enclosed a questionnaire which will take only a few minutes to complete and a postage-paid envelope for your mailing convenience. Your answers will be held strictly confidential and will be used only for research purposes. Should you have any questions at all about this request, please contact me at 757-680-1234.

Students at Margaret Elementary School would benefit tremendously from the experience of using their own computer. Will you offer them that possibility?

Sincerely,

Figure 31: The Persuasive Plan:
Sample Letter Set 2 for Persuading Your Reader

Letter 1:   NOT Using the Persuasive Plan

Dear Mr. Newark:

Please consider Ansend College when you are making charitable donations. This is one way to show your affection for and commitment to your alma mater.

Each year alumni contribute to Ansend College in meaningful ways. Whether volunteering at the Career Center, handling special events, or contributing financially, Ansend alumni continue to give back to their college.

Over the years, contributions have helped fund scholarships and improve campus technology. Annual gifts also benefit the College well after the dollars are earmarked. National foundations often use alumni participation as the basis for determining matching funds.

[. . . A sample letter like this might continue for 2 pages with factual information about donating.]

Congratulations to you for taking the time now to contribute to the Ansend Alumni Fund.

Sincerely,

Letter 2: _USING_ the Persuasive Plan

Dear Mr. Newark:

Each year Ansend College alumni contribute to their alma mater in meaningful ways. Whether volunteering at the Career Center, handling special events, or contributing financially, Ansend alumni show that they care. Last year, for example. . .

- _Dr. Kevin Crew ('89), a neurologist at Walter Reed Army Medical Center, returned to Ansend to speak with undergraduate students about preparation for medical school, applying to medical school, and finding research internships._

- _Ms. Sheryl Jonson ('92), a professional writer for Allied Corporation, assisted the Development Office in writing a grant that garnered scholarships for students with learning disabilities to receive specialized help from the campus writing center. Sheryl has a learning disability that did not stop her from achieving her goals at Ansend and beyond._

- _Mr. Jim Card ('58), a retired secondary school teacher, donated $1,000 toward exploratory programs for education on the Internet._

Will you join them this year?

Your contribution, no matter what size, can make a difference. Annual gifts also benefit the College well after the dollars are earmarked. Did you know that national foundations use alumni participation as the basis for determining matching funds?

Just five years ago, 21 percent of Ansend alumni made annual gifts to the College. Last year, 35 percent donated. In 1997, we're shooting for 40 percent participation. Will you become part of that 40 percent?

Please show that you care by completing the enclosed pledge card today or call 301-757-4321 now to find out how you can join Ansend in its efforts to provide a quality college experience.

Sincerely,

Critique of Sample Letter Set 2: The Persuasive News Message

Letter 1

The Persuasive Plan in Figure 25 asks you first to get the reader's attention, next to build interest and desire, then to ask the reader to take action. Letter 1 does not follow this plan. Instead, it opens with the action request: "Please consider Ansend College when you are making charitable donations. . . ." The letter does go on to provide factual information. In fact, as indicated, that information would cover a possible additional two pages. *(Remember that persuasive letters should be brief and to the point.)* Letter 1 also ends by congratulating the reader on having taken action rather than on asking for the action to be taken.

Letter 2

Letter 2 gets the reader's attention in its opening. It maintains reader interest by giving three examples of diverse ways that other readers have contributed. In addition, the examples involve real people that the reader is likely to identify with positively. It continues by building a desire for the reader to take action, and it closes with an action request. The four-part structure, as described in Figure 25, is *ATTENTION, INTEREST, DESIRE,* and *ACTION.*

Finally, remember when writing letters that the key to success involves analyzing your audience's and your own needs, maintaining an effective tone and style, and planning and adapting your material to fit the format required based on the type of information being sent: favorable, negative, or persuasive.

Letter Writing Exercises

(See Appendix B for exercises to improve your letter writing skills.)

CHAPTER 7

Memos: Traditional and Electronic

We often acknowledge the need to give special attention to letters since they leave the agency and affect our public image. Fewer people give necessary attention to memos since they are in-house documents. Generally, the feeling is that memos are less formal. However, in any business writing, your reputation is at stake. Prepare your memos carefully whether you are writing to the president of your agency, a co-worker, or a subordinate. Remember that memos are a critical representation of your professional self.

Traditional, hard-copy memos generally travel within the agency and are usually filed for documentation purposes. Electronic memos (e-mail) function quite differently from traditional memos in that e-mail is used between and among different agencies and often instead of the former traditional memo or letter. More information on e-mail will follow later in this chapter.

Whether using e-mail or a traditional memo, you must first consider your reader. As we have discussed with letter writing, analyze your reader's needs and your own purpose, and also analyze the reader's relationship to you. Do you want a more formal or a less formal tone? Certain word choices and use of contractions ("I don't" for "I do not") can alter levels of formality. See Chapters 4 and 5 for fuller discussion of tone and style. Remember to be sincere and credible in your communications.

Memo Formats

In the same way that three major types of letters exist, so do three types of memos. You can format your memos by using the same plans as those used for letters. (If you desire information about the typing of memos, please refer to Appendix B.)

Since memo writing typically involves general documentation of information rather than delivering of negative or persuasive news, you will find that the format for delivering positive or neutral news is used most frequently. Most memos are written in a deductive style with the main news first. Additionally, you will usually have a more established relationship with the reader of your memo than the readers of most of your letters. In Figure 32 both inductive and deductive formats are presented. Figure 33 then provides memo examples to illustrate the formats.

Figure 32: Two Orders Of Memo Messages

Order 1:
INDUCTIVE STYLE:

LEAST IMPORTANT DETAIL FIRST
followed by
Next Important Details
followed by
Conclusions and Recommendations

Order II:
DEDUCTIVE STYLE:

CONCLUSION AND RECOMMENDATIONS
followed by
Next Important Detail
followed by
Least Important Details

Effective business writers use the deductive style to write memos
UNLESS
the information being delivered is negative.

In order to understand the inductive and deductive formatting as described in Figure 32, let's take a look at a pair of memos in Figure 33. One memo is written in inductive format (the lesser details placed first, leading to the main details) and the other memo is written in deductive format (the main details placed first, followed by lesser details).

Figure 33: Sample Memo Set 1 Written in Two Styles

Memo 1: Inductive Style (Least to Most Important Details)

Date: September 22, 1997
To: Nursing Staff
From: Penelope Piedmont, R.N. *PP*
        Nursing Supervisor
Re: Important Emergency Room Meeting

Below I have listed emergency room statistics for the months of June, July, and August:
        June: 2,529 patients treated
        July: 2,321 patients treated
        August: 1,899 patients treated

The Emergency Room Committee is concerned with the decrease in number of patients treated over what our history indicates is usually our busiest time of year. There will be a mandatory meeting on Monday, September 30, at 9 A.M. in East Wing to address the committee's concerns. Thank you.

Memo 2: Deductive Style (Most to Least Important Details)

Date: September 22, 1997
To: Nursing Staff
From: Penelope Piedmont, R.N. *PP*
        Nursing Supervisor
Re: Important Emergency Room Meeting

You are asked to attend an Emergency Room Committee meeting on September 30 at 9 A.M. in East Wing. This meeting will address the concern of a decrease in number of patients treated over a three-month period. This period is considered historically to be the busiest time of year.

The following statistics indicate this decrease:
        June: 2,529 patients treated
        July: 2,321 patients treated
        August: 1,899 patients treated

If you have a schedule conflict, please contact me prior to September 28. Thank you.

Critique of Memos in Figure 33

The first memo requires that readers look over statistics without knowing why they are doing so. Even though the statistics may be of interest the first time, without a basis for reading them, readers will find it necessary to read the statistics again once they have finished reading the memo. Inductive style, or leading from the lesser to greater points, does not serve the reader well in this situation.

Notice that the deductive style in Memo 2 allows readers to understand before reading the statistics why they are reading them. A direct delivery allows the reader to have the main point in mind while secondary points are being presented. The deductive format should be used in any general memo delivery.

The deductive approach also works best when delivering voice mail messages. Have you ever received a lengthy voice mail message in which the sender supplies secondary details before supplying the main message? It is extremely difficult to listen to the information without a main point from which to understand the details. If the news is negative or persuasive in overall plan, using a less direct approach would be appropriate. If the news is general in nature, and most memo information as well as voice mail information is, the deductive or direct approach is best.

Let's look at a second example in Figure 34 comparing inductive and deductive styles.

Figure 34: Sample Memo Set 2 Written in Two Styles

Memo 1:   Inductive Style (Least to Most Important Details)

Date: November 2, 1997
To: Team Leaders
From: Liz Barbey *LB*
             Quincy Building Architect Senior
Re: Preparation for November 7 Meeting

I've enclosed for your consideration the blueprints for the proposed Quincy Building addition.

The meeting with Jackson Architect Associates is scheduled for Friday, November 7, at 8:30 a.m. in Quincy Hall.   If you have a schedule conflict, please contact me prior to November 5. Thanks.

Enclosure

Memo 2: Deductive Style (Most to Least Important Details)

Date: November 2, 1997
To: Team Leaders
From: Liz Barbey *LB*
             Quincy Building Architect Senior
Re: Preparation for November 7 Meeting

You are asked to attend the meeting with Jackson Associates on Friday, November 7, at 8:30 a.m. in Quincy Hall. This meeting will address the new addition to the Quincy Building. If you have a schedule conflict, please contact me prior to November 5.

I hope that reviewing the enclosed blueprints will help you to prepare for the meeting.

Enclosure

Critique of Memos in Figure 34

Memo 1 begins with information about the enclosed blueprints. What might happen in this case is that the reader will stop reading the memo and go directly to the blueprints. If this happens, the reader will miss valuable information about a meeting. Likewise, since the information in Memo 1 is inductive, the most important information—that about the meeting—is placed last and should be first.

In Memo 2, the most important information is presented first. Once the meeting date, time, and location are established, the writer then lets the reader know that the enclosed blueprints will be of assistance in preparing for the meeting. This order allows the reader to go directly to the blueprints after they are mentioned.

Action Memo Format

A specialized memo format, called the **action memo**, can be used when a memo must be written to document a problem that has occurred and a solution for handling it. This type of information frequently requires documentation. Using the action memo format allows the writer to place the information into a specific order that uses a more direct approach.

Typically in our academic writing assignments, we wrote essays that may have required us to explain an experience we had in which we learned a lesson. We rarely started with the lesson and then provided the details of the experience. Instead, we built the suspense of the story through a progression of the creative details. Using this type of approach can cause the reader to have to guess at the point while getting the details in chronological order. It will also create a lengthier memo in most cases.

The action memo format is traditionally a three-paragraph format. You may certainly alter this format to fit your own needs should you not have all the information indicated in the action memo outline.

Figure 35 provides the outline, and Figure 36 provides a sample memo illustrating its use. Notice how succinctly the information can be placed into three specific paragraphs.

Figure 35: Action Memo Format

Outline for the Action Memo

Paragraph 1: State the problem and its seriousness.
Present the solution.
Mention the cost, if any.

Paragraph 2: Discuss the cause(s) of the problem.

Paragraph 3: Present alternate way(s) of handling the problem.
Tell why those ways won't work or aren't the best solution.
End by repeating the solution and the action recommended.

NOTE: Sideheadings would be used to separate the paragraph sections as shown in Figure 36.

Figure 35 describes the three-paragraph format that places information in a specific order. In paragraph one, you state the problem that has occurred and tell why it is serious. You want to get the reader's attention so that he or she will listen closely to your solution and support it.

In paragraph two, you discuss the cause or causes of the problem. When did it occur? How? Why? Who was involved? Add all relevant details here. If you had begun the memo with these details, the reader may not have understood why he or she was reading them. By reading them in paragraph two, the reader understands how the details fit the picture.

In paragraph three, you present other options and tell why those options are not the best solution. It is important not to present only one solution, especially when you are seeking management approval. By presenting and discounting all the possible options, you will strengthen the solution that you recommend.

Let's take a look at
an action memo
that is written about
a printer problem at
a company called
"Enden." In this
situation, Enden
has developed a
printer that is not
compatible with
"Windows 95," and
this problem has
aroused negative
responses from
Enden customers.
As you read the
sample action
memo in Figure 36
written in response
to this situation,
note how it corre-
sponds to the
format in Figure 35.

Figure 36: Sample Action Memo

DATE: *January 4, 1997*
TO: *Matthew Frazer, Plant Supervisor*
FROM: *Courtney Leanne, Plant Operations Assistant CL*
RE: *Laser Printer 1400 Incompatibility with "Windows 95" Solution*

Problem, Seriousness, and Recommended Solution

*It has come to my attention that our Enden Printer Action Laser 1400
Model is not compatible with the "Windows 95" program. We have
received over 900 complaints about this printer for that reason, and I
believe that our reputation is at stake. I recommend that we offer clients
who have purchased the Enden 1400 model a pro-rated certificate that
could be applied toward the purchase of the Enden Action Laser 1600.
If clients do not want to purchase this printer, we can offer them $225 in
cash. The eligible clients for this rebate total approximately 5,000. The
cost will range from $1,125,000 to $1,500,000.*

Causes

*The 1400 Model printer is not able to print 32-bit applications properly.
The problem was caused by an oversight on the part of the development team. Clients believe that we knew that the printer would not
work with the program; therefore, they feel deceived. Over 900 complaints have been filed with Quality Assurance.*

Evaluation of Alternatives and Final Recommendation

I did evaluate other alternatives:
* *We could offer a full refund for the return of the purchased printer.
  (This is not in keeping with our original sales agreement, though, and
  the cost would be higher.)*
* *We could manufacture the component for the 32-bit application.
  (This is not feasible since it would seriously delay the development of
  our new product initiatives)*
* *We could offer the clients a 32-bit application called OS\3 made by
  IBR. (This would promote IBR over Macrosoft and could affect our
  relationship with Macrosoft.)*

*My recommendation is to offer clients a pro-rated certificate that could
be applied toward the purchase of the Enden Action Laser 1600 or the
offer of $225 in cash. This option allows us to maintain goodwill with
our clients and is the least costly option. I request that you approve
this recommendation so that we can begin to distribute the certificates.*

Critique of Sample Action Memo

In paragraph one, the writer begins with a statement of the problem—that the printer is not compatible with the "Windows 95" program. The writer then tells why this fact is serious—over 900 complaints have come in from customers, and the company's reputation is at stake. The writer continues by next recommending what she believes is the best solution—offering a pro-rated certificate or cash. The cost is mentioned last. (If a specific recommendation does not involve a cost factor, it would not be mentioned.)

Paragraph two reveals the causes of the problem. The language is clear and concise.

Paragraph three provides alternatives as well as a refutation for each alternative. Notice also that the writer effectively uses a list of bulleted items for ease of reading. (For further information on using lists, see Chapter 5.) The end of the paragraph requests approval of the recommendation presented in paragraph one. This provides a full circle development back to the beginning for further emphasis of the original solution.

Writing E-Mail Messages (Electronic Memos)

As mentioned, using **electronic memos** (or **e-mail**) has in some workplaces replaced the standard printed memo. Often, the e-mail message is considered to carry the versatility of a phone message (usually written and sent quickly). While some e-mail messages are extremely informal, such as confirming a pick-up time for a lunch date, it is important to remember that the e-mail message is not verbal; it is written. E-mail is often printed for documentation, and it is often sent to more than the one individual whom you intended to receive it. In fact, multiple receivers might read the e-mail message before the communication has ended. Since you do not know where the message may end up, especially if the message is work-related, you should pay careful attention to grammar, mechanics, and presentation of the message. It must be written with care and attention to professionalism.

E-mail messages should follow the general formats discussed in regard to memos; however, because e-mail messages require the reader to view them on a screen, they warrant certain rules of usage. Figure 37 contains general rules of e-mail usage, Figure 38 contains a sample e-mail message, Figure 39 presents key components of the e-mail message, and Figure 40 supplies notations used frequently by e-mail writers.

Figure 37: General Rules of E-Mail Usage

Electronic memos:

- ***Need to be tightly organized*** *so that related contents appear in "sections." Screens are usually limited to 24 or fewer lines. It is easier for readers to see related material together than to scroll through the message to find information.*

- ***Communicate their major contents early*** *(like effective printed memos). It's best not to add unnecessary details that will make the reading more difficult. Remember that the e-mail reader doesn't have the convenience of seeing the entire message at once unless it is printed. He/she may also reject the message after reading the first section. Also, readers of e-mail messages may require more time and may experience greater difficulty in looking at multiple screens.*

- ***Require more explicit subject lines*** *than printed memos. Remember that readers of e-mail memos use the subject line to decide whether to read the message. If the subject line is vague (for example, "meeting"), the reader may not understand the specific topic.*

- ***Need sideheads*** *within them to help readers understand the sections as they scroll through the document.*

- ***Should indicate to the reader that an additional page is coming.*** *This is important if the reader is reading from a terminal or terminal emulation. Symbols such as >> or :more: are used to signal this to the reader. In addition, some writers also let the reader know when the end has been reached by providing symbols such as # # # or :**END**:.*

- ***Are not secure.*** *It is false to assume that your e-mail message is private. Not only can it be read by someone on your network, but if you are sending e-mail over the Internet, your transmission can be intercepted and read by anyone who knows how to manipulate the system. Unless you are sure that extraordinary precautions have been taken to keep the e-mail private, you should assume that the mail is not secure.*

- ***Can be retrieved often when they have been deleted.*** *All communications leave "electronic footprints" that a trained specialist can follow. Therefore, do not put in an e-mail message information that you would not want to have read by someone else or printed.*

- ***Should not be written in all capital letters*** *since it may appear to the reader as though you are shouting.*

- ***Should be written with careful attention to grammar, mechanics, usage, and spelling*** *in the same way that printed memos are written. You will appear to your reader to be less credible as a writer and as a professional if you do not attend to this careful check.*

Critique of Sample E-Mail Message (Figure 38)

From:	**Todd M Replogle**
	[SMTP:treplo@mosaicnet.com]
Sent:	*Monday, March 17, 1997 5:51 PM*
To:	*cynthia@exis.net*
Subject:	*Upcoming Planning Meeting on March 24*

Meeting on March 24

Cynthia, the Planning Committee of Project B will be meeting on Monday, March 24, at 3:00 p.m. at Heritage Center Suite 202. We plan to address a number of agenda items but still hope to keep the meeting to one hour. I have included the proposed agenda below. Please call before March 19 if you are unable to attend.

Agenda

The following agenda items include both standard and new business to be covered:

I.   Approval of Minutes of March 10 Meeting (Distributed Previously)

II.   Old Business: Garcy Development Approval

III.   New Business
A.   Parking Problem on Hampton Boulevard and Proposed Solutions
B.   Brecht Award

IV.   Adjournment

I hope to see you on March 24.

All the Best,

Todd

Notice that this e-mail message closely resembles an ordinary memo in a deductive format. The major information regarding the meeting is supplied first; then the agenda (much like an attachment) is supplied next. One difference that you find here is the use of sideheads (*Meeting on March 20* and *Agenda*) that help to break up the text. Sideheads make e-mail easier to follow visually since they help to organize the material. Also, note the use of the agenda list. Again, the list helps to break up the text and to make the material easier to follow. In e-mail, it is important to remember that the readers are reading from a screen, not a written sheet, so using sideheads as well as lists can help to make the material easier to follow.

E-Mail Format Considerations

E-mail messages are often less formal in tone than printed memos and are often written with less regard for convention. E-mail messages also are often composed and sent quickly. These reasons do not mean that you need to be less careful with your writing of e-mail. Pay attention to all conventional rules of effective writing. Keep your message short and emphasize key parts of the message by using sideheads and lists in the message text when possible.

Figure 39 describes the key components of the e-mail message. While certain e-mail programs may vary slightly, the following components are fairly standard.

E-Mail Abbreviations and Symbols

Figure 40 provides symbols and abbreviations of the e-mail writer. Frequent users of electronic mail often become familiar with e-mail jargon to speed up the efficient use of language in their messages. These writers may abbreviate common expressions or add emotion to messages by using nonverbal symbols. Use e-mail jargon ONLY if you are sure that your reader understands it. Many people feel that e-mail jargon is better suited for personal rather than for professional messages.

Figure 39: Key Components of the E-Mail Message

Component	Description	Use
From:	*Your name and e-mail address.*	*Use for accurate identification and delivery.*
Sent:	*Date and time.*	*Some programs include this information automatically.*
To:	*Recipient's e-mail address and/or screen name*	*Use for accurate identification and delivery.*
Subject:	*Description of e-mail message content.*	*Use to help the reader decide the reading priority. Be specific to aid the busy reader.*
cc:	*Person or persons to receive a copy of your message.*	*Use as appropriate.*
Attachments:	*File name of additional information being sent.*	*Use as appropriate.*
Message:	*E-mail information being transmitted.*	

Figure 40: Standard Abbreviations and Symbols of the E-Mail Writer

E-Mail Abbreviations	
bcnu	be seeing you
btw	by the way
fwiw	for what it is worth
fya	for your amusement
fyeo	for your eyes only
fyi	for your information
imo	in my opinion
lol	laughing out loud
msgs	messages
nlt	no later than
obtw	oh, by the way
pres	presentation
ptp	pardon the pun
rec'd	received
thx	thanks
tmrw	tomorrow
rgds	regards
pls	please

E-Mail Symbols	
:-) or :)	grin or smile
;-) or ;)	wink
:-(or :(	frown
:-D	laugh
:-*	kiss
:-o	shocked
:-X	sealed lips
:-ll	angry
:'(	sad or crying
:-<	very upset
8-)	wide-eyed

E-Mail Etiquette

People frequently ask my opinion regarding standard rules for e-mail etiquette. The following points might prove helpful for both senders and receivers:

Sender Etiquette

- Decide whether e-mail is the best method to use to deliver your message.

- If you are angry, be sure not to send a message that expresses your anger. Give yourself time to cool down since once your message is sent, you cannot retrieve it.

- Keep e-mail messages short and well organized.

- Limit the use of e-mail jargon and symbols, and use them only with a reader who understands them.

- International messages require sensitivity to differences in culture and language.

- Send personal messages from your company system only if your agency permits it.

- Ask permission before you forward anyone else's message no matter what length the message is.

- Do not copy the sender's message in your reply (even if it is copied automatically by your system) unless the sender's message is important for reference. Save from it what you need and trim what you do not need. This will save your reader time.

- Send messages only to people who need or have requested or expressed interest in your information. Remember that each message received creates work for the recipient.

- Don't put an "urgent" note on a message that is not urgent since your receiver may not believe you the next time.

- Send e-mail messages with careful attention to grammar and mechanics as well as format and style.

Receiver Etiquette

- Decide whether e-mail is the best method for your reply.

- Reply to messages in a timely manner. Some messages may not warrant a reply.

- If you are angered by a message, be sure not to respond too quickly. Give yourself time to cool down since once the message is sent, you cannot retrieve it.

- Do not copy the sender's message in your reply (even if it is copied automatically by your system) unless the sender's message is important for reference. Save from it what you need and trim what you do not need.

- When you reply to a sender, be sure that you maintain the context of the sender's message. In other words, don't reply with a "yes" since the sender may have forgotten the question or information that was sent.

Final Comments

Prepare your memos carefully whether e-mail or traditional memo format. First, analyze your reader's needs and your own purpose as well as analyze the reader's relationship to you. Organize your message well and pay attention to grammar and mechanics. Remember that how well you present yourself in writing is a part of your professional image. Be sincere and credible in all of your communications.

Memo Writing Exercises

(See Appendix C for exercises to improve your memo writing skills.)

CHAPTER 8

Choosing the Right Word: Proper Usage

Usage refers to word choice. For example, do I choose "affect" or "effect" in the following sentence: "What (affect, effect) will my behavior have on Joe?"

In business, proper or standard usage is critical for two primary reasons:

- Incorrect use can cause confusion and miscommunication.

- Errors reflect on how you are perceived as a professional.

Your writing credibility reflects your professional credibility. If a person receives a memo that contains a usage error, rarely does that person say, "Oh, well, I suppose Janice just didn't have time to proof closely." Rather, the person is likely to consider Janice to be careless or not concerned about her professional image.

Spellchecker, the computer device that most of us have grown to rely upon, will only check spelling errors. Many usage errors are not caused by misspelling. After all, in the sentence above, "affect" and "effect" are both spelled correctly.

The most important thing a concerned writer can do is to brush up on usage skills.

In order to check your usage skills, complete the following exercise in this chapter by circling what you consider to be the right choices. Answers to the exercise are found in Appendix D, and information to help you understand commonly confused words follows this exercise.

Exercise 8-1: Choose what you consider to be the correct choice. Compare your answers to those found in Appendix D for this exercise.

1. The speaker (accidently, accidentally) fell over the podium.

2. (Who's, Whose) ready to go to dinner?

3. I will (accept, except) your invitation to dinner.

4. I would like (a half, half a, a half a) piece of pie.

5. That rule is (altogether, all together) irrelevant in this situation.

6. (You're, Your) personal life is none of my business.

7. It was (already, all ready) four o'clock before we realized it.

8. "Breathe deeply" was the coach's (advise, advice).

9. (A, An) employee responded to the supervisor's question with (a, an) example.

10. Exact figures often (allude, elude) me.

11. She had difficulty deciding (among, between) the three dresses which one to buy.

12. They readily (ascented, assented) to our suggestions.

13. Let me (assure, insure) you that I will report the problem immediately.

14. This (device, devise) was invented by a surgeon.

15. (Besides, Beside) the beautiful lake was a field of flowers blooming.

16. The pen is indeed mightier (than, then) the sword.

17. It was as though her dream had (bust, busted, burst).

18. Her report (affected, effected) a change in departmental policy.

19. Her friend's attitude (affected, effected) her deeply.

20. The father's behavior had serious (affects, effects) on his son's attitude.

21. (Can, May) I give your child a free (desert, dessert)?

22. He (can hardly, can't hardly) keep up the pace.

23. The (data, datum) were analyzed carefully.

24. Franklin Street was the (site, sight, cite) of the accident.

25. This (coarse, course) fabric scratches my skin.

26. During those two hours beverages are (complimentary, complementary).

27. When she became (conscious, conscience) of her feelings, her (conscious, conscience) bothered her.

28. He (could care less, couldn't care less) about his homework.

29. The number of items (is, are) unpredictable.

30. A number of items (is, are) unpredictable.

31. You (could of, could've) done a better job.

32. The one (criteria, criterion) that the chemist used for that test is clear.

33. Fortunately, the judge is (disinterested, uninterested) in every case brought before her.

34. The (Capital, Capitol) is in Washington, D.C.

35. I couldn't believe that the preacher would engage in such an (elicit, illicit) activity.

36. Elizabeth is an (eminent, imminent) speaker on that topic.

37. How much (farther, further) he will drive depends upon how tired he becomes.

38. There should be (fewer, less) than ten cups of coffee in that pot.

39. Ms. Wagner performed (good, well) in the role of Nora.

40. I (have, have got) one week to write the report.

41. They should take care of (theirself, theirselves, themselves).

42. Her attitude (implies, infers) that she is angry.

43. (In regards to, In regard to) the chapter message, I am lost.

44. (Irregardless, Regardless) of the reason, I am disappointed.

45. (It's, Its) a gorgeous day outside, so I will let the dog out of (it's, its, its') doghouse.

46. The instructor will (learn, teach) the students about protons.

47. (Let's us, Let's) decide on a place to eat before we (lose, loose) our appetites.

48. Our last day to work here (maybe, may be) coming soon.

49. (Alot, A lot) of trouble can be avoided by following directions.

50. It's (alright, all right) with Bob Bonner.

51. What is the (moral, morale) of that story?

52. She did as well on the test as (myself, me, I).

53. We thought that time (passed, past) very slowly that day.

54. The (Personal, Personnel) Department handles all employee issues.

55. It was based on one (phenomena, phenomenon).

56. The high school (principal, principle) tried to instill in the student body certain (principals, principles) of behavior.

57. We (quit, quite, quiet) advertising the item since it caused (quit, quite, quiet) a stir.

58. Sharon ran into the office and (says, said), "Let's eat!"

59. Please secure that podium so that it is (stationary, stationery) on the platform.

60. Well, (then, than), does he plan to go?

61. (There, Their, They're) not attending the lecture that is held (their, there, they're).

62. I will speak (to, too, two) you in the morning since I am (to, too, two) upset now.

63. "Yes, this is (he, him)."

64. While many workers (emigrated, immigrated) from Mexico during the 1970's, many Mexicans (emigrated, immigrated) to the United States.

65. Of the items you've mentioned, I prefer the (later, latter).

66. We (adapted, adopted) the guidelines to our needs.

67. Be (sure and, sure to) consult a lawyer.

68. Only my little finger was (broke, broken).

69. I considered becoming an engineer, an artist, and an architect, (respectively, respectfully).

70. Our coins (use to, used to) contain silver.

71. The wedding begins at ten in the (a.m., morning).

72. The advertisement was (explicit, implicit): "All Sales Final."

73. (Almost, Most) everyone agreed with the proposed changes.

74. Her co-worker's (continuous, continual) questions prevented LaShawna from finishing her project on time.

75. The manager was (discreet, discrete) about the employee's reasons for absence.

STANDARD USAGE
Commonly Confused Words

A, An: Use <u>a</u> before a consonant sound.
>   *A nuclear war, **a** happy client*
Use <u>an</u> before a vowel sound.
>   ***An** owl, **an** honest mistake*

Accept/Except: <u>Accept</u> is a verb meaning to agree to something or to receive something.
>   *I will **accept** her offer.*
<u>Except</u> is a preposition indicating that something is to be left out.
>   *I will attend the conference **except** for the opening session.*

Accidentally/   The correct spelling is <u>accidentally.</u>
Accidently: >   *I **accidentally** overheard their discussion regarding his promotion.*

Adapt/Adopt/   <u>Adapt</u> means to change usually to fit.
Adept: >   *I will **adapt** the regulations to fit our situation.*
<u>Adopt</u> means to take on.
>   *I will **adopt** your leave policy for use by my department.*
<u>Adept</u> is an adjective meaning skilled.
>   *The director is **adept** at handling questions from various groups.*

Advice/Advise: <u>Advice</u> is a noun.
>   *The counselor offered me **advice.***
<u>Advise</u> is a verb.
>   *My professor will **advise** me on my topic.*

Affect/Effect: <u>Affect</u> is a verb meaning to influence or to change.
>   *The child's feelings **affect** my decision.*
<u>Effect</u> is a noun indicating a result.
>   *What **effect** will the child's feelings have on your decision?*
<u>Exception</u>: Use effect in the phrase "effect a change."
>   *The outcome of the meeting **effected** a change in departmental procedure.*

Ain't: Unless it is used for a humorous effect, the word "ain't" should be avoided since it is considered to be nonstandard.

Allude/Elude: <u>Allude</u> is a verb that means to make an indirect reference.
>   *The candidate has **alluded** to a new campaign slogan.*
<u>Elude</u> is a verb that means to evade or escape from.
>   *The suspect has tried to **elude** the FBI.*

Allusion/Illusion: <u>Allusion</u> refers to an indirect reference.
> *The preacher made an **allusion** to an afterlife.*

<u>Illusion</u> refers to a false impression or an unreal image.
> *The video game was full of optical **illusions.***

Almost/Most: Using <u>most</u> as a substitute for <u>almost</u> is considered too informal--especially in business writing.

Alot/A lot: The correct spelling is <u>a lot.</u>
> ***A lot** of time is wasted in excessive planning.*

Already/All ready: <u>Already</u> means "before or by the time of."
> *The meeting has **already** begun.*

<u>All ready</u> means "fully prepared."
> *The committee members were **all ready** to get started.*

Alright/All right: <u>Alright</u> is a common misspelling for <u>all right.</u>

Altogether/ All together: <u>Altogether</u> means "completely."
> *His response was **altogether** too detailed for his audience.*

<u>All together</u> means "in a group."
> *The children's drawings were arranged **all together** on the bulletin board.*

Among/Between: <u>Among</u> is used for more than two items.
> ***Among** her ideas was the addition of office space.*

<u>Between</u> is used for only two items.
> ***Between** you and me, I am pleased with the outcome.*

<u>Note</u>: **Between you and me is correct.** *Do not use "between you and I."*

A.M./P.M. (or a.m./p.m.): Use only with figures, for example, 7:30 a.m. or 7:30 A.M.
> *The event begins at 7:30 a.m. and ends at 4:30 p.m.*

And etc.: Avoid using <u>and etc.</u> Etc. (Et cetera) means "and so forth." <u>And etc.</u> is redundant.

Anyone/Any one: <u>Anyone</u> means any person at all.
> ***Anyone** can perform that activity.*

<u>Any one</u> refers to a specific person or thing in a group.
> ***Any one** of those children might buy a lunch.*

<u>Note:</u> Similar forms are **everyone/every one** and **someone/some one.**

Anyways/ Anywheres: Nonstandard language: Use **anyway, anywhere.**

Ascent/Assent:	<u>Ascent</u> means to rise or to climb or the act of something rising.
	*The road has an **ascent** of ten degrees.*
	<u>Assent</u> means to agree.
	*They readily **assented** to our suggestions.*
Assure/Ensure/ Insure:	These words are similar in meaning in that each one means to make certain. Usage follows:
	<u>Assure</u> means to make a person sure of something.
	*Let me **assure** you that I will report the error immediately.*
	<u>Ensure</u> and insure are used to mean a guarantee against harm or failure.
	*Donations are necessary to **ensure** that there is an adequate budget.*
	<u>Insure</u> is used more frequently with technical guarantees about property or life.
	*Are you **insured** against property damage?*
At:	It is considered nonstandard to use <u>at</u> after <u>where</u>.
	AVOID: *Where does she live at?*
	USE: *Where does she live?*
Awhile/A while:	<u>Awhile</u> is an adverb and cannot be the object of a preposition.
	*Stay **awhile.***
	<u>A while</u> is composed of an article and a noun. It can be the object of a preposition.
	*Stay for **a while.***
Be sure and:	Use <u>be sure to</u> instead of <u>be sure and</u>.
	***Be sure to** let me know your opinion.*
Beside/Besides:	<u>Beside</u> means "next to."
	*She worked with the tape player **beside** her desk.*
	<u>Besides</u> means "except" or "in addition."
	*No one **besides** Bruce is allowed to do that.*
	*Charlotte has another part-time job **besides** her full-time employment.*
Between/Among:	See **Among/Between.**
Broke/Broken:	<u>Broke</u> is the past tense of "break."
	*He **broke** his arm in the accident.*
	<u>Broken</u> is used as a past participle of break.
	*The cookie was **broken** by the hungry child.*
	<u>Broke</u> is a nonstandard choice as a past participle of break and is acceptable only in informal use to mean without money.
	*After the election, the Republicans were **broke.***
Burst, bursted, bust, busted:	<u>Burst</u> is the standard form while the other three are considered to be slang.
	*The helium balloon **burst.***

But what:	Nonstandard language. Use <u>that</u> instead of <u>but what.</u>
	  AVOID: *Samantha has no doubt **but what** her job will be terminated.*
	  USE: *Samantha has no doubt t**hat** her job will be terminated.*

Can/May:	The word <u>can</u> is traditionally reserved to mean ability.
	  ***Can** you juggle three oranges without dropping one?*
	<u>May</u> is used to refer to permission.
	  ***May** I help you?*

Can't Hardly/ Can Hardly:	<u>Can't hardly</u> is a double negative. Use <u>can hardly.</u> *He **can hardly** hear me because of the street noise.*

Capital/Capitol:	<u>Capital</u> means major one or chief one. Each state has a capital city.
	It can also refer to money or to upper case letters.
	  *It was a decision of **capital** importance.*
	<u>Capitol</u> refers to the primary building in Washington, D.C., or other primary buildings of government.
	  *The **Capitol** in Washington, D.C., is being renovated.*

Cite/Site/Sight:	<u>Cite</u> refers to pages, ideas, and progress that are cited or noted.
	  *She was **citing** the Bible in her own book.*
	<u>Site</u> refers to a place.
	  *Franklin Street was the **site** of the accident.*
	<u>Sight</u> refers to one of the five senses.
	  *His **sight** of distant objects is failing.*

Climactic/Climatic:	<u>Climactic</u> is derived from climax, the point of greatest intensity.
	  *The **climactic** years during the Queen's reign occurred during the late 1800's.*
	<u>Climatic</u> is derived from climate.
	  *The **climatic** conditions leading to the hurricane are being studied.*

Coarse/Course:	<u>Coarse</u> means jagged or rough.
	  *This **coarse** fabric is uncomfortable to wear.*
	<u>Course</u> refers to a plan, a topic, a course of study.
	  *Claudette is doing well in her paralegal **course.***

**Compliment/
Complement:**
	<u>Compliment</u> means an expression or act of praise or courtesy.
	  *The guests **complimented** the host on the beautiful table arrangements.*
	<u>Complement</u> means to complete.
	  *The silver tray **complements** the decor nicely.*

**Conscience,
Conscious:**
	<u>Conscience</u> is a noun meaning "moral principles."
	  *Use your **conscience** as your guide.*
	<u>Conscious</u> is an adjective meaning "aware" or "alert."
	  *Was he **conscious** of Bill's admiration for him?*

Continuous/ **Continual:**	Continuous means without stopping. *The clock on the shelf **continuously** ticks.* Continual means steady but with brief interruptions. *The student used the library computer **continually** throughout the semester.*
Could care less/ **Couldn't care less:**	Could care less is a nonstandard expression. Use couldn't care less instead. *The child couldn't care less about her homework.*
Could of/Could've:	Could've is the correct spelling of the contraction for could have. *The children **could've** won a prize if they had known the answer.*
Criterion/Criteria:	Criterion is singular and means a test or rule. *The one **criterion** that the chemist used during the experiment was clear.* Criteria is plural and means a number of such tests or rules. *He based his research method upon varied **criteria.***
Data/Datum:	Data refers to facts that are often gathered during an investigation. The term is technically plural. *The **data** were analyzed carefully.* Datum refers to a point, line, or surface used as a reference, for example, in surveying or mapping. It is the singular form. *The surveyor indicated the **datum.***
Desert/Dessert:	Desert refers to sand. *The **desert** was at an unbearable temperature.* Desert also refers to abandon. *The lover **deserted** her friend.* Dessert refers to sweets eaten often after a meal. *Mary hasn't eaten her **dessert.***
Discreet/Discrete:	Discreet means being careful about what you say or do. *The manager was **discreet** about the employee's reason for illness.* Discrete means to divide things into separate components. *The child performed two **discrete** homework tasks.*
Disinterested/ **Uninterested:**	Disinterested means impartial, not biased. *The judge is **disinterested** in the case.* Uninterested means not interested. *I am **uninterested** in her excuse for procrastinating.*
Done:	Be careful of your use of the word "done." Use standard English. AVOID: *That record is **done** sold. Do you know who **done** it?* USE: *That record has sold. Do you know who did it?*

Don't/Doesn't: Use these words appropriately according to standard English.
  AVOID: *She **don't** know the answer.*
  USE: *She **doesn't** know the answer.*

Each and Every: This phrase is redundant. Use one word or the other.

Effect/Affect: See **Affect/Effect.**

Elicit/Illicit: Elicit means to gain information, to bring or draw out.
  *His questions **elicit** valuable information in the case.*
  Illicit means unlawful or illegal.
  *His fortune was a result of **illicit** sales.*

Emigrate/Immigrate: Emigrate is a verb meaning to leave one country or region to settle in another.
  *His grandparents **emigrated** from Mexico that year.*
  Immigrate is a verb meaning to enter or settle in a country or region that is not native.
  *His grandparents **immigrated** to the United States.*

Eminent/Imminent: Eminent means well known or famous.
  *Groucho Marx was an **eminent** comedian.*
  Imminent means that something is about to happen.
  *An **imminent** storm is approaching rapidly.*

Everyone/Every one: See A**nyone/Any one.**

Explicit/Implicit: Explicit means fully and clearly expressed.
  *The sales slogan was **explicit**.*
  Implicit means understood (or implied) though not directly expressed.
  *There was an **implicit** agreement not to mention that item.*
  Implicit can also mean having no doubts or reservations.
  *He had **implicit** trust in his boss' decision.*

Except/Accept: See **Accept/Except.**

Farther/Further: Farther refers to distance (remember the word *far* in *farther*).
  *That store is **farther** away than I thought.*
  Further refers to more.
  *She will give it **further** consideration.*

Fewer/Less: Fewer refers to number, to something countable; less refers to degree.
  ***Fewer** students attended that lecture.*
  ***Less** information was provided by the instructor on that day.*

Good/Well: Good is an adjective; well is an adverb.
  AVOID: *Mr. Murphy plays the guitar **good**.*
  USE: *Mr. Murphy plays the guitar **well**.*

Half a, A half, A half a: Use <u>half a</u> or <u>a half,</u> but avoid <u>a half a.</u>
                             AVOID: *They worked **a half a** day.*
                             USE: *They worked **a half** day.*
                                         *They worked **half a** day.*

Has Got/Have Got: <u>Got </u>is unnecessary in this construction:
                             AVOID: *I **have got** one week to write this report*
                             USE: *I **have** one week to write this report.*

Hisself/Theirself: These are not words. Substitute **himself** or **themselves**.

Illicit/Elicit: See **Elicit/Illicit.**

Illusion/Allusion: See **Allusion/Illusion.**

Immigrate/Emigrate: See **Emmigrate/Immigrate.**

Imminent/Eminent: See **Eminent/Imminent.**

Imply/Infer: The person communicating the message can <u>imply</u> (suggest without stating) while the reader or listener <u>infers</u> (reaches a conclusion).
                             *Her attitude **implies** that she is angry.*
                             *Her friends **infer** from her comments that she may resign.*

In regards to: Nonstandard: Use <u>in regard to</u> or <u>as regards.</u>

Incidentally/Incidently: The correct spelling is <u>incidentally.</u>
                             ***Incidentally**, I will be attending the meeting on Thursday.*

Incredible/Incredulous: <u>Incredible</u> means too extraordinary to be believed.
                             *Gary always told **incredible** stories.*
  <u>Incredulous</u> means inclined not to believe.
                             *Marie was **incredulous** when Gary mentioned the thirty-foot snake.*

Inferior than: Nonstandard: Use <u>inferior </u>to or <u>worse than.</u>

Irregardless: Nonstandard: Use <u>regardless.</u>

Is When/Is Where: Do not use "when" and "where" after "is" when providing definitions.
                             AVOID: *Breathwork i**s when** the person breathes with a trained coach and moves energy in the body.*
                             USE: *Breathwork is a type of therapy that involves coached breathing that moves energy in the body.*

Its/It's: <u>It's</u> can be used only as a contraction for <u>it is</u> or <u>it has.</u>
                             ***It's** a problem that occurs frequently.*
  <u>Its</u> can be used only to indicate the possessive.
                             *The cat licks **its** fur.*

Later/Latter/Last: Later refers to time and is the comparative form of late.

*He will call you **later**.*

Latter refers to the last named of two items.

*I prefer the **latter** item mentioned.*

Last is used if more than two items are mentioned.

*The **last** item in the set was broken.*

Lay/Lie: Learn when to use lie and lay. The following chart may help:

Present (Infinitive)	Past Tense	Past Participle	Present Participle
(To) lie	**lay**	**lain**	**lying**
(To) lay	**laid**	**laid**	**laying**

To lie means to rest in a horizontal position. To lay means to put or place something somewhere. As a rule, the word lay usually takes an object.

*I will **lie** in the sun on Saturday.*

*She **had laid** the book aside while she spoke.*

Learn/Teach: Learn means to gain knowledge while teach means to impart knowledge.

*The instructor will **teach** the students about protons.*

*The student who pays attention will **learn** a great deal.*

Less/Fewer: See **Fewer/Less.**

Let's us: Redundant for let's. Let's is a contraction for let us.

Lose/Loose: Lose is a verb meaning to no longer have.

*Will he **lose** your respect?*

Loose is an adjective meaning not fastened.

*That bolt is **loose**.*

May be/Maybe: May be is the verb form.

*Our last day to work here **may be** coming soon.*

Maybe is the adverb meaning perhaps.

***Maybe** our last work day will be coming soon.*

Moral/Morale: Moral is the noun meaning a lesson or maxim.

*What is the **moral** of that short story?*

Morale is the noun that refers to a state of mind.

*The staff's **morale** is low due to budget cuts.*

Most/Almost: See **Almost/Most.**

Myself (also Himself/Herself):	<u>Myself</u> is used as an intensive or reflexive pronoun. *I, **myself**, will take responsibility for the work.* *I must decide for **myself**.* Avoid using myself as a substitute in general for I or me. AVOID: *She did as well on the test as **myself.*** USE: *She did as well on the test as **I** (did).* AVOID: *The counselor encouraged my friend and **myself**.* USE: *The counselor encouraged my friend and **me**.*
Nohow/ Nowheres:	Nonstandard. Use <u>not at all</u> for <u>nohow</u>. Use <u>nowhere</u> for <u>nowheres</u>.
Of:	The preposition <u>of</u> is nonstandard when substituted in writing for the verb form <u>have</u>. AVOID: *Fontelle **could of** (would of, should of, might of, may of, must of) done that yesterday.* USE: *Fontelle **could have** (would have, should have, might have, may have, must have) done that yesterday.*
Off of:	In standard writing omit the <u>of</u>. AVOID: *He fell **off of t**he roof.* USE: *He fell **off** the roof.*
Only/Onliest:	The word <u>onliest</u> does not exist in standard usage.
Past/Passed:	<u>Past</u> indicates the time before now. *That occurred in the **past**.* <u>Passed</u> is the past tense of the verb "pass"— to move along. *The time **passed** very slowly.*
Personal/Personnel:	<u>Personal</u> means private. *Her feelings were **personal**.* <u>Personnel</u> refers to the individuals employed by an agency. *Non-essential **personnel** were allowed to arrive at work later as a result of the treacherous road conditions.*
Phenomenon/ Phenomena:	<u>Phenomenon</u> is the singular of the word meaning "an occurrence." *A similar **phenomenon** occurred the night before.* <u>Phenomena</u> is the plural form of the same word. *Strange **phenomena** occur frequently on those premises.*

Principal/Principle: Principal is an adjective or noun meaning "chief" or "head official."
*The high school **principal** says that she is your "pal."*
*The **principal** reason that the student failed was poor attendance.*
Principal is also a noun referring to the capital or main body of an estate or a financial holding as distinguished from the interest or revenue from it; also a sum of money owed as a debt, upon which interest is calculated.
*The interest calculated on the **principal** was sizable.*
Principle is a noun meaning "rule." (Notice that principle and rule both end in -le.)
*The speaker tried to impart the meaning of the **principle** of life.*

Proceed/Precede: Proceed means to continue, to go forth.
*Business **proceeded** as usual.*
Precede means to go ahead, to surpass, or to be earlier than something else.
*She **preceded** her specialized lecture with an effective graphic.*

Quit/Quite/Quiet: Quit means to end something.
*The store **quit** advertising that product.*
Quite is an adverb meaning a great deal.
*The boss is **quite** upset by your attitude.*
Quiet is the adjective meaning the opposite of noisy.
*The library was **quiet** that afternoon.*

Reckon: Nonstandard: Use guess or think.

**Residence/
Residents:**   Residence refers to the place in which one lives.
Residents refers to people who live in a specific location.

**Respectfully/
Respectively:**   Respectfully means "full of respect."
*He submitted the report **respectfully** to the chair.*
Respectively means "in the order given."
*I would like to become a teacher, a researcher, and a writer, **respectively**.*

Says/Said: Be careful not to interchange these words.
Says is present tense.   Said is past tense.
AVOID: *Sharon ran into the office and **says**, "Let's eat."*
USE: *Sharon ran into the office and **said**, "Let's eat."*

Somewheres: Nonstandard: Use somewhere.

**Stationary/
Stationery:**   Stationary means "in a fixed position."
*The table was **stationary**.*
Stationery refers to paper, particularly letterhead.
*The office **stationery** was quite impressive with its new design.*

**Statue/Statute/
Stature:**   Statue is a piece of sculpture.
*The **statue** stood in the park adorned by ivy.*
Statute is a legal restriction.
*The paralegal course covers material related to **statutes**.*
Stature refers to someone's size.
*That young boy was small in **stature**.*

Than/Then:	Do not interchange these words.
	Than is a conjunction used in comparisons.
	*He is taller **than** his brother.*
	Then refers to time.
	*At first, my sister decided to take her vacation in July; **then** she decided that April would be a better month.*
Their/There/ **They're:**	Their is a possessive pronoun.
	***Their** obsession with money was suspect.*
	There is an adverb or an expletive.
	***There** are many books on that subject.*
	They're is the contraction for "they are."
	***They're** not about to change their minds.*
Theirself/Themself/ **Theirselves:**	Nonstandard: Use themselves.
To/Too/Two:	To is the preposition.
	*I will speak **to** you in the morning.*
	Too is the adverb meaning "too much" or "also."
	*She is **too** upset to speak now. Her friend is upset, too.*
	Two refers to the number.
	***Two** children exited the corridor.*
Toward/Towards:	Toward and towards are interchangeable; however, toward is the preferred usage.
Try and/Try to:	Try and is informal for try to. Use try to.
	AVOID: *Elizabeth will **try and** study if she has time.*
	USE: *Elizabeth will **try to** study if she has time.*
Use to/Suppose to:	Nonstandard expressions: Use used to and supposed to. Be sure to add the -d.
	*You are **supposed to** do it the way it **used to** be done.*
Well/Good:	See **Good/Well**.
Who/Which:	Use who or that instead of which to refer to people. Use which to refer to things.
	*That bus patrol was the one **who** told her **which** seat to occupy.*
Who's/Whose:	Who's can always be replaced with "who is."
	***Who's** responsible for that project?*
	Whose is a possessive pronoun.
	***Whose** committee is responsible for the report?*
You was:	Nonstandard: Use you were.
You're/Your:	Your is the possessive pronoun.
	***Your** best option is the larger monitor.*
	You're is a contraction for "you are."
	***You're** on the right track.*

CHAPTER 9

How to Avoid the Five Major Grammar Errors That Writers Make

Grammar refers to a generally agreed-upon set of rules or a norm that prescribes the current standard for how words combine to form sentences. While Appendix A provides grammar terms and definitions that you may find helpful, this chapter is devoted to five major grammar errors that deserve attention:

- **Fragment**

- **Comma Splice**

- **Fused Sentence (or Run On)**

- **Subject-Verb Disagreement**

- **Pronoun-Antecedent Disagreement**

These errors create confusion and are often considered to weigh more heavily in terms of writer credibility than other more minor mistakes.

FRAGMENT

A fragment is an incomplete sentence. It is usually a group of words that begins with a capital letter and ends with a period but lacks a complete grammatical structure. As a rule, do not use sentence fragments in business writing.

To be complete, a sentence must have a subject and a verb. In the following sentence, the subject (S) and the verb (V) are indicated.

S   V
The **employee took** four leave days.

A fragment is a structure that can be incomplete because
- It has no subject.
     Was turning his telescope skyward.
     (Revised: Chin Li was turning his telescope skyward.)
- It has no verb.
     Chin Li turning his telescope skyward.
     (Turning is not a complete verb. Revised: Chin Li was turning his telescope skyward.)
- It has no subject and no verb.
     Through his telescope.
     (Revised: Through his telescope, Chin Li focused on the star.)
- It is a dependent clause.
     When Chin Li turns his telescope skyward.
     (When is a subordinator, a word that creates dependency. Either remove the subordinator or add an independent clause.)
     (Possible Revisions: When Chin Li turns his telescope skyward, he can see the stars. OR Chin Li turns his telescope skyward.)

To revise a fragment, add the missing element until you have a complete sentence with a subject and a verb. Before sending off any business document, including an e-mail message, proofread to avoid fragments.

The following business examples contain fragments and possible revisions:

Fragment: Mr. Morales spoke to me about the Turney case. And for days tried to influence my decision.

Revision: Mr. Morales spoke to me about the Turney case and for days tried to influence my decision.

    Mr. Morales spoke to me about the Turney case. In fact, for days he tried to influence my decision.

Fragment: A few days later. The payment arrived in a badly torn envelope.

Revision: A few days later, the payment arrived in a badly torn envelope.

Desirable Fragments: Some types of fragments are considered acceptable and standard. Look at the following examples:

- **Exclamation:** I will not go. Not ever!

- **Questions and Answers:** Why? Because the policy indicates a limit of ten days.

Written dialogue that mirrors speech often contains fragments as in the following example:

- **Dialogue:** "Oh, yes. My briefcase holds the essential items."

COMMA SPLICE

A *comma splice* is an error involving improper comma use between two main clauses. Each main clause (or subject-verb unit) is independent requiring a stronger mark of punctuation than a comma to separate them. Avoid two main clauses which are separated by a comma only.

Comma Splice: Her back was injured, she could not go to work.

You may revise a comma splice in a number of ways:

Put a period: Her back was injured. She could not go to work.

Put a conjunction: Her back was injured, and she could not go to work. (Conjunctions: and, but, or, nor, for, so, yet)

Put a semicolon: Her back was injured; she could not go to work.

Make one clause a dependent clause: Because her back was injured, she could not go to work.

Note that comma splices can also arise when a comma is used with a conjunctive adverb between main clauses. A conjunctive adverb is an adverb that is used to connect or relate main clauses. The following is a list of conjunctive adverbs:

accordingly	also	anyhow	besides	consequently
furthermore	hence	henceforth	however	indeed
instead	likewise	meanwhile	moreover	nevertheless
otherwise	still	then	therefore	thus

Comma Splice: Her back was injured, therefore, she could not go to work. (In this example, the comma before the conjunctive adverb "therefore" between main clauses creates the comma splice.)

You may revise in a number of ways:

Put a period: Her back was injured. Therefore, she could not go to work.

Put a semicolon: Her back was injured; therefore, she could not go to work.

FUSED SENTENCE (RUN ON)

A **fused sentence** is an error that results when two main clauses are run together with no punctuation. Avoid two sentences which have no mark of punctuation between them. (Be careful not to insert a comma and to create a comma splice.)

FUSED (RUN ON):   Her back was injured she could not go to work.

You may revise as follows:

Put a period:	Her back was injured. She could not go to work.
Put a conjunction and a comma:	Her back was injured, so she could not go to work.
Put a semicolon:	Her back was injured; she could not go to work.
Make one clause dependent:	Because her back was injured, she could not go to work.

To test your knowledge of these three errors, do the following exercise based on examples from actual business writing. Answers are found in Appendix D.

Exercise 9-1: Fragment, Comma Splice, Fused Sentence Errors

On the line to the left, identify the error in each example as fragment, comma splice, or fused sentence. Correct the error. If an example is correct, indicate that.

_____1. Believing that you will want an analysis of sales for November. We have sent you the figures.

_____2. She asked me to research the latest standards for pricing, therefore, I did so quickly.

_____3. He declared that such a procedure would not be practical. And that it would be costly also.

_____4. This campaign will help sell Widener products the outcome looks promising.

_____5. Generally speaking. Profits are at an all time high.

_____6. A possible refund was recommended, however, it would go against policy.

_____7. The new contract provides substantial wage increases, the original contract emphasized shorter hours.

_____8. The flood damaged much of the equipment in Building 21. Making it necessary to stop production.

_____9. Cork or asbestos sheeting must be hand-cut; polyurethane may be poured into a mold.

_____10. The new model is being introduced this year it is designed for the adventurous.

AGREEMENT

Agreement refers to the correspondence in number (singular with singular and plural with plural) between subjects and verbs. It also refers to the correspondence in number and gender (feminine with feminine, masculine with masculine, and neuter with neuter) between pronouns and their antecedents. The antecedent is the word that the pronoun refers to (for example, <u>Vicky</u> is the antecedent for <u>her</u> in the sentence "<u>Vicky</u> had a great deal on <u>her</u> mind.")

Subject-Verb Agreement:	*Sandra has a new job.* (Singular subject *Sandra* with singular verb *has*)
Pronoun-Antecedent Agreement:	*Mohammed always carries his briefcase to work.* (Singular pronoun *his* with singular antecedent *Mohammed*)

SUBJECT-VERB AGREEMENT RULES

The verb in a sentence agrees in number with the subject, not with intervening words. Do not let nouns in prepositional phrases, for example, influence your choice of verb form. The following rules and examples will supply you with important information about subject-verb agreement.

1. Do not make errors because of nouns or pronouns coming between the subject and the verb or because of subjects and verbs with endings difficult to pronounce.

   *The excellent **condition** of the stamps **helps** to sell them.*
   *Every **one** of you **is invited** to the luncheon.*
   ***Scientists structure** the research data.*

2. As a rule the number of the subject is not changed by additional expressions beginning with words such as *accompanied by, along with, as well as, in addition to, including, no less than, not to mention, together with.*

   *The **singer** as well as the musicians **is invited** to the dance.*
   *The **musicians** as well as the singer **are invited** to the dance.*

3. Subjects joined by <u>and</u> are usually plural.

   *My **parents** and **<u>my uncle</u>** do not understand me.*
   Exception: My friend and sister, Ms. Dayna Bischof, is very creative. ("Friend and sister" refers to the same person.)

4. When <u>every</u> or <u>each</u> comes before singular subjects joined by <u>and</u>, use a singular verb.

   ***Every** cup, plate, and saucer **has** to be counted.*
   Placed after a plural subject, <u>each</u> does not affect the verb form.
   *The **dog and the cat** each **have** their own habits.*

5. Use a singular verb for singular subjects joined by <u>or</u>, <u>either/or</u>, or <u>neither/nor</u>.

   <u>Either</u> the **mayor** <u>or</u> the **governor is** the featured speaker.

6. If one subject is singular and one is plural, the verb agrees with the nearer subject.

*The quality nor the **prices have changed.***
*The prices nor the **quality has changed.***

7. Watch inverted word order (Verb + Subject) or the structure There + Verb + Subject which may cause you to make a mistake in agreement.

*Hardest hit by the high prices **were** American **tourists**.*
*Among our grandest ideas **is** the **concept** of an infinite universe.*
*There **were** Vietnam War **protests** and civil rights **marches**.*

8. When used as subjects, words such as <u>each</u>, <u>either</u>, <u>neither</u>, <u>one</u>, <u>everybody</u>, and <u>anyone</u> regularly take singular verbs.

***Each** of my colleagues **does have** political ambitions.*
***Everybody** in the choir **has** tickets to the harvest ball.*

9. Collective nouns should take singular verbs when they refer to the group as a unit and take plural verbs when they refer to individuals or parts of the group. (Almost 99% of the time collective nouns are singular in form.)

*My f**amily has** its traditions.*
*That **committee is** meeting on Monday.*

10. A linking verb should agree with its subject, <u>not</u> with its complement (predicate noun).

*His **complaint is** missed opportunities.*
*Missed **opportunities are** his complaint.*
*Excessive **absences were** the reason for her failure.*
*The **reason** for her failure **was** excessive absences.*

11. Some nouns require different forms of agreement depending upon their use.

***Athletics is** mandatory for every student.*
(The word "athletics" here implies a course of study.)
***Athletics provide** good muscle toning.*
("Athletics" here implies the varied sports.)

PRONOUN-ANTECEDENT RULES

Pronouns and their antecedents must agree in number and in gender. Pronouns take the place of nouns. Antecedents are the words to which pronouns refer. Pronoun-antecedent agreement is the correspondence between a pronoun and its antecedent in number (singular with singular, plural with plural) and in gender (feminine pronoun with feminine antecedent, masculine with masculine, neuter with neuter). The following rules and examples will supply you with important information about pronoun-antecedent agreement.

1. A singular antecedent (one that would take a singular verb) is referred to by a singular pronoun; a plural antecedent (one that would take a plural verb) is referred to by a plural pronoun.

   An employee *during training learns* **his or her** *role.*
   Employees *during training learn* **their** *roles.*

2. Use a singular pronoun to refer to such antecedents as <u>each</u>, <u>either</u>, <u>neither</u>, <u>one</u>, <u>anyone</u>, <u>everybody</u>, a <u>person</u>, and so on.

   Each *of these companies had* **its** *records audited.*
   One *has to live with* **oneself.**
   A **person** *has to live with* **himself or herself,** *but* **people** *have to live with* **themselves**.

3. Two or more antecedents joined by <u>and</u> are referred to by a plural pronoun.

   Courtney and Lauren *lost* **their** *self-confidence.*
   He and she *have* **their** *problems to resolve.*

4. Two or more singular antecedents joined by <u>or</u> or <u>nor</u> are referred to by a singular pronoun.

   Did **Courtney or Lauren** *lose* **her** *self-confidence?*

5. If one of the two antecedents joined by <u>or</u> or <u>nor</u> is singular and one is plural, the pronoun usually agrees with the nearer antecedent.

   Neither the **package** *nor the* **letters** *had reached* **their** *destination.*
   Neither the **letters** *nor the* **package** *had reached* **its** *destination.*

6. Collective nouns are referred to by singular or plural pronouns, depending on whether the collective noun is used in a singular or plural sense. (Approximately 99% of the time, the collective noun is singular. Be sure to be consistent with verbs and pronouns.)

Inconsistent:	*The* **choir** <u>is</u> *writing* **their** *own music.*
Consistent:	*The* **choir** <u>is</u> *writing* **its** *own music.*
Inconsistent:	*The* **group** <u>does</u> *not agree on methods, but* **they** *unite on aims.*
Consistent:	*The* **group** <u>does</u> *not agree on methods, but* **it** *unites on aims.*

The following exercise will help you evaluate your ability to use both subject-verb agreement and pronoun-antecedent agreement appropriately.

Exercise 9-2: Agreement Errors

This exercise tests subject-verb and pronoun-antecedent agreement errors. In each sentence, circle what you consider to be the correct choice. Answers to this exercise can be found in Appendix D.

1. Our branches in Hawaii (stock, stocks) different items.

2. There (is, are) the existence of phobias for which there is no explanation.

3. The fear associated by the individual with death experiences (is, are) tragic.

4. The term "opportunities" (has, have) been defined as a chance for advancement.

5. The definition given in many dictionaries (cover, covers) the term well.

6. Nancy and Jim (has, have) their issues to work out.

7. Each manager in all the departments (has, have) requested a raise this year.

8. The jack and the hubcap (was, were) missing.

9. Every one of you (is, are) invited to join us this evening.

10. Either the statue or the hanging plant (adorn, adorns) the entrance.

11. His problem (is, are) frequent financial losses.

12. If any one of the sisters needs a ride to church, (she, they) can call me.

13. Stray kittens or even an abandoned grown cat has (its, their) problems.

14. Neither of them ever asks for a second helping; (he/she, they) (is, are) too full.

15. The books or the periodical is appropriate in (its, their) use.

16. The Washington team was opportunistic in (its, their) plight.

17. If everybody minded (their, his/her) own business, life would be more pleasant.

18. Each person has a right to do what (he/she, they) (wants, want).

19. The committee is determined to make (their, its) stand on the issue tomorrow.

20. Paula or her secretaries will answer the phone if (she, they) can.

Avoid Sexist Language with Pronouns

Plural pronouns do not have gender (for example, "they"). Singular pronouns have three genders: masculine, feminine, and neuter. While the masculine pronoun was acceptable formerly in general usage to refer to any person, today the use of "he" is considered unacceptable when the gender of the antecedent might be either male or female.

Sexist:	A **dentist** who treats **his** patients well is generally respected in the community.
Nonsexist:	A **dentist** who treats **his** or **her** patients well is generally respected in the community. (Note that the phrase **her or his** could also be used.)

To avoid gender-specific pronouns, change the wording in a sentence from singular to plural:

Nonsexist: *Dentists who treat **their** patients well are generally respected in the community.*

You may also try avoiding the pronoun altogether:

Nonsexist: *Dentists who treat patients well are generally respected in the community.*

The issue of sexist writing is a critical one. As a businessperson, you need to be aware of the guidelines that will enable you to use gender-neutral language in your writing.

Use gender-neutral terms whenever possible.

Figure 41: Using Gender-Neutral Terms

AVOID	USE
mankind	humankind, people, human beings, humanity
layman	layperson
fireman	firefighter
policeman	police officer
foreman	supervisor
manpower	workforce, staff
craftsman	craftsperson
to man	to staff, to operate, to run, to work
manhours	workhours
the working man	worker, working people
one-man show	one-person show
forefathers	ancestors
workmen's compensation	worker's compensation
businessman	businessperson
chairman	chairperson, chair

As a rule, avoid the overuse of "she/he," " he/she," and "his/her." These words often look awkward and may sound awkward. **Instead, use "he or she" and "his or her." You may also try to reword the antecedent to use plural pronouns if possible.**

Treat women and men fairly when referring to them.

Sexist language treats women and men differently often without conscious reason. Do you treat people equally when referring to them? Some women find that they are referred to by their first names while males in the same context are not. Be consistent. Note the following example:

Sexist: The chair of the Sociology Department is Mona Danner, and the chair of the Faculty Senate is Professor Jones.

Nonsexist: The chair of the Sociology Department is Mona Danner, and the chair of the Faculty Senate is Ralph Jones.

Nonsexist: The chair of the Sociology Department is Professor Danner, and the chair of the Faculty Senate is Professor Jones.

Exercise 9-3: Gender Awareness

Revise the following sentences according to the principles of gender awareness.
Suggested answers are found in Appendix D.

1. Each employee must meet with his supervisor to discuss his performance appraisal.

2. It is Nancy's job to man the desk during the lunch break.

3. I do not think that workman's compensation will cover your medical bills.

4. Each manager should submit his monthly report.

5. The chairman of every committee at that university is involved in the planning process.

6. Dr. Thomas is our keynote speaker, and Victoria Spalding will provide our opening address.

7. According to the eighth grade teacher, each student will be given enough time to look over his material before taking the quiz.

8. Every writer should be aware of his audience while beginning the writing process.

9. Every businessman will benefit from the rigorous exercises in the new book.

10. Extreme courage is required of every fireman.

General Communication Guidelines

Writing effectively requires knowledge and a little patience. The tools provided in this book will help you to write more clearly while using your own natural writing voice to maintain a professional tone. The following guidelines describe the overall process:

1. As the sender, analyze your **audience** (the receiver) carefully. Consider the receiver's situation and perspective BEFORE sending the message. Also, pay attention to the different levels of audience that you encounter. What are the reader's abilities and needs?

2. Decide on your **purpose** in communicating. What are you trying to do? Are you trying to inform, persuade, convince, promote goodwill? Know your purpose in each of your written works and work to achieve your goal while staying aware of the reader's needs.

3. Consider carefully the best **method**, or medium, of communication. Should your message be spoken or written? Should you send a traditional memo or an e-mail message? Is a letter required? If so, what format should you use? The method you use to communicate will help to shape the document.

4. Send your message with care, whether verbal or nonverbal, written or spoken, with attention to **clarity**. Consider your language. Do you want highly generalized vocabulary or low-level generalized? In other words, *is tool* a better word choice than *implement* given this audience? Are your specialized terms clear to this reader?

5. Strive to have an effective **tone**—one that is natural, tactful, positive, and personal. Your tone is the attitude that you convey to your reader. Strive for an attitude that will allow you to be heard and understood without any negative impact on the reader. Be sincere and credible in your communciations.

6. Are your sentences concise or too wordy? Notice the methods mentioned in this book for improving the **style** of your writing.

7. Pay attention to **feedback** received. When you are speaking, the feedback you receive is generally immediate.   Your listener's nonverbal response (for example, nodding of the head) can help you to adjust your delivery. When you write, the feedback is often delayed. You do not hear from your reader immediately in most cases. Whether immediate or delayed feedback is given, pay close attention to your feedback. Adjust your delivery as needed. For example, is your reader telling you that he or she doesn't understand your use of specialized terms? If so, define more carefully.

8. Strive for **shared meaning**. The ultimate goal of any communication is shared meaning between sender and receiver. If you regard your own needs as most important, you may fall short of meeting the reader's needs. Work toward a balance in your communication, being sure that all needs are met.

9. Be **sensitive** to others, particularly to cultural differences. Remember that not all people use the same general thought process, have the same cultural history and experiences, understand the same analogies, or use the same expressions. Part of your planning process in writing requires carefully considering who your reader is and being sensitive to individual needs.

10. Make sure that your writing is **grammatically and mechanically correct.** Errors in spelling, usage, grammar, and mechanics reflect poorly on any writer, no matter what his or her status. No one is exempt from the need to use conventional writing standards.

Grammar Assistance

BASIC GRAMMAR TERMS THAT CAN BE HELPFUL

Noun: Person, place, thing, idea, object.
     Examples: employee, Yonkers, desk, courage, disk

Verb: Expresses action, condition, or state of being.
     Examples: studies, is, were, reads, becomes

Pronoun: Takes the place of a noun.
     Examples: I, she, he, it, they, you, we, them, us, me, etc.

Antecedent: A noun or pronoun to which a pronoun refers.
     Examples: *Susan* walked into the room and took her seat.
                 Everyone is invited to bring his or her friend to the party.

Adjective: Describes a noun or pronoun.
     Examples: *two* pages, *beautiful* picture, *useful* guide

Adverb: Describes a verb, adjective, or other adverb.
     Examples: wrote *carefully*, spoke *well*, *very* good idea

Conjunction: A connecting word.
     Examples:
     Coordinating conjunctions: and, but, or, nor, for, so, yet
     Subordinating conjunctions: when, if, since, because, etc.
     (Subordinators cause dependency in structures. See Chapter 9 on fragments.)

Conjunctive Adverb: A transitional word.
     Examples: therefore, thus, for example, for instance,
                 however, consequently, and so on
     (NOTE: *Beware of punctuation with these words so that you do not create a comma splice.* Refer to Chapter 9.)

Interjection: Expresses exclamation.
     Examples: Yes! Wow! Gee! Bravo!

Preposition: A function word that indicates relationship.
     Example: to, at, by, with, on, in, for, etc.

Object: Follows and receives the action in a sentence. You can usually determine the object by asking "what" or "whom" after the verb or preposition.
     Example: He protested the *strike*. (what)
                 She went to the store with *him*. (whom)

Subject: The person, thing, or idea that the sentence is about; a fundamental part of a sentence.

Example: The cautious *worker* put on his hard hat.

Sentence: A group of words that includes a subject and a verb and expresses a complete thought.

Example: In our organization, meetings are necessary to ensure company interaction.

Clause: A group of related words that contains a subject and a verb. Two types of clauses are independent (main) and dependent (subordinate).

An independent clause can stand alone as a sentence.
Example: Birds fly.
A dependent clause cannot stand alone and does not express a complete thought.
Example: When birds fly. *(When creates dependency.)*

Phrase: A group of related words that does not contain a subject or verb and that does not express a complete thought.

Examples: On the table   During the discussion

Exercise A-1: *Identifying Grammar Terms in a Passage*

Read the following brief passage, and identify the parts of speech as requested.
Answers can be found in Appendix D.

Passage:
Information on budgeting effectively and on recording carefully is provided for you in this inexpensive guide. Wow!

1. What is the subject?   _____

2. What is the verb?   _____

3. Name one preposition: _____

4. Name one pronoun: _____

5. Name one interjection: _____

6. Name one conjunction: _____

7. Name one adverb: _____

8. Name one adjective: _____

GRAMMAR'S TOP VERB ERRORS

Today I:	Yesterday I:	In the past, I have:	Today I:	Yesterday I:	In the past, I have:
am (from to be)	was (we were)	been	lie	lay	lain
become	became	become	mistake	mistook	mistaken
begin	began	begun	ride	rode	ridden
bend	bent	bent	ring	rang	rung
bet	bet	bet	run	ran	run
bite	bit	bitten (or) bit	see	saw	seen
bleed	bled	bled	seek	sought	sought
blow	blew	blown	send	sent	sent
bring	brought	brought	shake	shook	shaken
burst	burst	burst	shine	shone	shone
buy	bought	bought	shrink	shrank	shrunk
cast	cast	cast	sing	sang	sung
choose	chose	chosen	sink	sank (or) sunk	sunk
cling	clung	clung	slide	slid	slid
cost	cost	cost	speak	spoke	spoken
dig	dug	dug	spin	spun	spun
dive	dived (or) dove	dived	spring	sprang	sprung
drink	drank	drunk	sting	stung	stung
drive	drove	driven	stink	stank	stunk
fling	flung	flung	strike	struck	struck
fly	flew	flown	swear	swore	sworn
forbid	forbade	forbidden	swim	swam	swum
forget	forgot	forgotten	swing	swung	swung
freeze	froze	frozen	take	took	taken
get	got	gotten	tear	tore	torn
grind	ground	ground	think	thought	thought
hang	hung	hung	throw	threw	thrown
have	had	had	wake	woke	waken
hurt	hurt	hurt	weep	wept	wept
know	knew	known	wind	wound	wound
lay	laid	laid	wring	wrung	wrung
lend	lent	lent			

PREPOSITIONS

A prepositional phrase consists of a preposition and its object and possibly modifiers of the object. It is helpful to know common prepositions since the subject of a sentence is not found in a prepositional phrase. (See Chapter 9 for further information.)   Some of the common prepositions, with examples of phrases, are the following:

about	(about the room)
above	(above the desk)
after	(after the show)
among	(among the people)
around	(around the roadblock)
at	(at the museum)
before	(before noon)
beside	(sitting beside Donna)
besides	(no one besides Kim is coming)
between	(between you and me)
by	(by the stream)
concerning	(concerning your answer)
down	(down the street)
during	(during the storm)
for	(for Fleta Jackson)
from	(from Claudette Johnson)
in	(reading in the library)
in front of	(in front of an audience)
inside	(inside the room)
into	(stepping into the room; not stepping in the room)
like	(like Robert)
of	(of the chosen ones)
off	(fell off the table; not fell off of the table)
over	(over the curb)
through	(through the crowd)
to	(to a meeting)
together with	(together with a co-worker)
toward	(toward the wall)
under	(under the table)
until	(until the break)
with	(with the group)

USING COMMAS EFFECTIVELY: THE BASICS

Rules for Using Commas

Comma Rule #1: Use a comma to prevent misreading.

When the bullet struck, Mary Francis screamed.
When the bullet struck Mary, Francis screamed.

Comma Rule #2: Use a comma before *and, but, or, nor, for, so,* and *yet* when they link main clauses.

Webster may renew his license for one year, or he may renew for two years.
No one watches the facilitator, for everybody is taking notes.

Comma Rule #3: Use a comma after introductory elements (for example, long phrases, transitional expressions).

When Americans are not spending money, they feel dissatisfied.
Intelligent he was not. In fact, he barely passed the course.

Comma Rule #4: Use commas to separate items in a series (including coordinate adjectives).

The flag was red, white, and blue. (A comma before "and" is optional.)
Kim Fisher is a gracious, loving therapist.

Comma Rule #5: Use commas to set off nonrestrictive clauses and phrases and other miscellaneous elements. (*Nonrestrictive* refers to information that does not restrict the main meaning.)

Preparation for the final exam, as my student has pointed out, will require a great deal of studying.

Comma Rule #6: Use commas to set off nonrestrictive elements, contrasted elements, geographical names, and items in dates and addresses.

My piano instructor, Ms. Martha Hayward, is a talented musician.
Skating is supposed to be a show of skill, not an exercise in danger.
Leonardtown, Maryland, is the site of her birth.
The letter was addressed to Ms. Dolores Morgan, St. Louis, Missouri 19938.
Joe applied for the job in July 1994 and accepted it on Friday, August 5, 1994.

Rules for Avoiding Unnecessary Commas

Comma Error #1: When the dependent clause follows the main clause, there is usually no need for a comma.

    NO: He won, because he would not give up.
    YES: He won because he would not give up.

Comma Error #2: Do not set off restrictive elements with a comma.

    NO: My daughter will not eat anything, containing onions or pickles.
    YES: My daughter will not eat anything containing onions or pickles.

Comma Error #3: Do not use a comma to separate the subject from the verb or the verb from its object.

    NO: Even students without true financial need, can apply for financial aid.
    YES: Even students without true financial need can apply for financial aid.
    NO: The student said, that the test was difficult.
    YES: The student said that the test was difficult.
    YES: The student said, "That test was difficult."

Comma Error #4: Do not misuse a comma before or after a coordinating conjunction.

    NO: The clothes were selected, and washed with care.
    YES: The clothes were selected and washed with care.
    NO: Mary Johnson, and Martin Novelle were among the award recipients.
    YES: Mary Johnson and Martin Novelle were among the award recipients.

Comma Error #5: Do not use a comma before the first item or after the last item of a series (including coordinate adjectives.)

    NO: Books were required for certain topics, such as, health, geology, and biology.
    YES: Books were required for certain topics, such as health, geology, and biology.
    NO: The society caters to talented, ambitious, energetic, students.
    YES: The society caters to talented, ambitious, energetic students.

Exercise A-2: Comma Self-Check

Add or remove commas as needed. If a sentence is correct, indicate that.
Answers can be found in Appendix D.

1. Although Gary preferred Marie Marvin was chosen.

2. That flag has green yellow and red stripes.

3. Bonita, and Ahmad were both prepared to interview.

4. My grandparents' new address is Route 2 Box 39-B Compton Maryland 20650.

5. Preparing the department budget as my boss has told me will be quite time intensive.

6. The reason is, that the dress is too elegant to wear.

7. The armed forces excelled, on the ground, and in the air.

8. I was shocked that Tandora quit her job since I thought that she was comfortable with her workload.

9. The work may take two hours or it may take only one hour.

10. Even with gloves on his hands and a hat on his head he was still cold.

Business Letter and Memo Parts and Typing Formats

The appearance and layout of business letters and memos are important to the image you are conveying. Appropriate presentation enhances your professional image. While most companies have their own stationery as well as standard letter or memo typing format, Appendix B provides the traditional information on this subject.

Standard Parts of the Letter

Heading   The heading consists of your address. If you are using company stationery, the heading consists of your company name, address and possibly phone, fax, and e-mail numbers.

Date   The date consists of the month, day, and year. In general, do not abbreviate the month or add *st, th,* or *nd* to the day:
July 14, 1997   or   14 July 1997

Inside Address   The inside address consists of the name and address of the individual to whom you are writing. It usually includes that person's official title (such as Personnel Director or President), the name of the agency, and the complete address. It may also include a courtesy title, such as Ms., Mr., Miss, Mrs., or Dr.

In general, you should spell out street addresses (Avenue or Drive); however, states may be abbreviated. Be sure to use the correct post office abbreviation for each state. (See the list of abbreviations at the end of this appendix.) Remember to include the zip code. The person's title may appear on the same line as the name or may appear below the name.

Ms. Michelle Kelley, Manager   *Ms. Michelle Kelley*
Spirituality Products, Inc.   *Manager*
92961 Kozoyed Lane   *Spirituality Products, Inc.*
Chesapeake, Virginia   23456   *92961 Kozoyed Lane*
                                              Chesapeake, Virginia 23456

Attention Line   The attention line is optional. You may use the attention line to direct your information to a certain person or department. The attention line appears below the inside address. Usually the attention line replaces the salutation. The attention line may also be placed on the envelope.
Attention: Joseph Jesse Cryer
Attention: Quality Assurance Department

Salutation   The salutation matches the first line of the inside address. If your inside address reads Joseph Jesse Cryer, the salutation would read Dear Mr. Cryer or Dear Joseph, depending on your level of formality. While the salutation is usually followed by a comma in a personal letter, the salutation is followed by a colon [:] in a business letter. If you do not know the sex of the individual to whom you're writing (for example, Dana Chlan), do not guess. Instead, you may use Dear Dana Chlan as your salutation.

If you do not know the name of the recipient, you may use *Dear Sir or Madam* or *Dear Madam or Sir* or you omit the name altogether by using a salutation such as *Greetings!* Depending on the type of correspondence, you may also use salutations such as *Dear Search Committee* or *Dear Editor.*

Subject Line

The subject line may be used to highlight the purpose or subject of the letter. Even though it is written to direct attention to the subject, it may also be used for filing purposes. The subject line opens with the word Subject and is followed by a colon and an information line. The subject line appears usually directly below the salutation line and is most often capitalized.

SUBJECT: PROPOSAL RESPONSE NUMBER 541988

Body

The body forms the message of the letter. Single-space the body but double-space between paragraphs.

Complimentary Close

The complimentary close appears after the body of the letter and is usually followed by a comma. Only the first word is capitalized.

Sincerely,   *Respectfully submitted,*

Signature

Sign your name in the space below the complimentary close and above your typed name. Your signature indicates that you are endorsing the message. All letters, even those mass produced, should carry a signature.

Writer's Name and Title

Your name and title should appear below the handwritten signature.

Mark Banes, Vice President
Family Services Bureau

Reference Initials

Reference initials are standard when letters are typed by a secretary. The writer's initials appear in capitals followed by a colon or slash and the typist's initials in lowercase letters.

CLJ:mmw   *CLJ/mmw*

Reference initials are omitted if the writer is the typist.

| **Enclosure Line** | If you have enclosures that accompany your letter, you would indicate this by the word Enclosure or Enclosures or the abbreviation Enc. below the reference initials. You may also describe the enclosure. |

Enclosure: Contract   *Enc.: Contract*

| **Copy Line** | If copies of the letter are being sent to other readers, this can be indicated by the notation cc or c as desired.   The colon is optional. |

cc: Liz Zielinski   *c: Liz Zielinski*   *cc Liz Zielinski*

If a blind copy is being sent to a second reader, the notation bcc or bc is used. **NOTE:** The *bcc* or *bc* notation is placed on the copy of the letter that is sent to the second person; however, it is NOT placed on the original letter. The recipient to whom the letter is addressed will not know that the bcc recipient exists.

| **Postscript** | A postscript, usually indicated by P.S., is more common in personal letters than in business letters. Avoid using postscripts too frequently. They may imply that the letter was poorly planned. |

| **Second Page Letter Heading** | The second and successive pages of a business letter should be indicated as such for identification purposes. This identification includes the name of the person being addressed, the page number, and the date. The information may be placed vertically or horizontally. |

Mr. Matthew Frazer
Page 2
April 1, 1997

Mr. Matthew Frazer   -2-   *April 1, 1997*

| **Typing Styles** | Two standard letter typing styles are provided in this appendix: *full block, modified block,* and *semi-block letter style.* While other styles exist, these are the most popular business letter typing styles. |

Example 1: Full Block Letter Style

POWELL INFORMATION SYSTEMS
4816 Chipstead Drive
Emporia, Virginia 23920
757-789-1234 (Phone)
757-789-1235 (Fax)

"Experience the Power of Powell"

May 4, 1997

Mr. Richard Corbin, President
Corbin and Company
1029 Donna Lane
Virginia Beach, Virginia 23432

Dear Mr. Corbin:

Thank you for the excellent instruction you provided me in your course "Being in Business." The valuable material in each session helped me to evaluate my business situation and to make important decisions.

I look forward to applying your "principles of business success" as I continue to explore new opportunities. The time and personal attention you provided me is greatly appreciated.

Sincerely,

Angela Powell

Angela Powell, President

AP:lf

cc: Robert Widener

P.S. Congratulations on moving into your new home. I wish you all the best.

Example 2: Modified Block Letter Style

TOWN POINT PARKING GARAGE

1210 St. Paul's Boulevard
South Bend, Indiana 23509
(219) 555-5789

April 17, 1997

Ms. Karen Fletcher, President
Fletcher and Associates
22 Quest Drive
South Bend, Indiana   23505

Dear Ms. Fletcher:

SUBJECT: PARKING SPACE AVAILABILITY

Thank you for your interest in renting a parking space at the Town Point
Parking Garage. A monthly rental space is available at a rate of $29.95 per
month with unlimited hours in the southern wing of the main parking garage,
Lot B, on Henderson Avenue.

The enclosed contract provides further details. If you agree to the terms
explained in the contract, please sign as indicated on page 3, and return the
contract in the enclosed postage-paid envelope. Should you have any
questions, please feel free to call me at 555-5789.   I would be happy to
answer your questions.

Sincerely,

Frank Friedland

Frank Friedland, Administrator
Town Point Parking Department

FF/td

Enclosure: Parking Contract

Example 3: Semi-block Letter Style

TOWN POINT PARKING GARAGE

1210 St. Paul's Boulevard
South Bend, Indiana
23509
(219) 555-5789

April 17, 1997

Ms. Karen Fletcher, President
Fletcher and Associates
22 Quest Drive
Norfolk, Virginia   23505

Dear Ms. Fletcher:

SUBJECT: PARKING SPACE AVAILABILITY

Thank you for your interest in renting a parking space at the Town Point Parking Garage. A monthly rental space is available at a rate of $29.95 per month with unlimited hours in the southern wing of the main parking garage, Lot B, on Henderson Avenue.

The enclosed contract provides further details. If you agree to the terms explained in the contract, please sign as indicated on page 3, and return the contract in the enclosed postage-paid envelope. Should you have any questions, please feel free to call me at 555-5789.   I would be happy to answer your questions.

Sincerely,

Frank Friedland

Frank Friedland, Administrator
Town Point Parking Department

FF/td
Enclosure: Parking Contract

Two-Letter Mailing Abbreviations

United States

State	Abbreviation	State	Abbreviation	State	Abbreviation
Alabama	AL	Kentucky	KY	Oklahoma	OK
Alaska	AK	Louisiana	LA	Oregon	OR
Arizona	AZ	Maine	ME	Pennsylvania	PA
Arkansas	AR	Maryland	MD	Puerto Rico	PR
California	CA	Massachusetts	MA	Rhode Island	RI
Colorado	CO	Michigan	MI	South Carolina	SC
Connecticut	CT	Minnesota	MN	South Dakota	SD
Delaware	DE	Mississippi	MS	Tennessee	TN
District of Columbia	DC	Missouri	MO	Texas	TX
		Montana	MT	Utah	UT
Florida	FL	Nebraska	NE	Vermont	VT
Georgia	GA	Nevada	NV	Virginia	VA
Guam	GU	New Hampshire	NH	Virgin Islands	VI
Hawaii	HI	New Jersey	NJ	Washington	WA
Idaho	ID	New Mexico	NM	West Virginia	WV
Illinois	IL	New York	NY	Wisconsin	WI
Indiana	IN	North Carolina	NC	Wyoming	WY
Iowa	IA	North Dakota	ND		
Kansas	KS	Ohio	OH		

Canada

Province	Abbreviation	Province	Abbreviation
British Colombia	BC	Nova Scotia	NS
Labrador	LB	Ontario	ON
Manitoba	MB	Prince Edward Island	PE
New Brunswick	NB	Quebec	PQ
Newfoundland	NF	Saskatchewan	SK
Northwest Territories	NT	Yukon Territory	YT

Standard Parts of the Memo

Common Memo Parts   Although memo formats vary from one organization to another, most
have several parts in common: date, to, from, subject, or reference line.

DATE:

TO:

FROM:

SUBJECT:

The headings may be arranged in one column as shown above or may be
arranged in two columns:

TO: FROM:

DATE: SUBJECT:

The order of the items may vary. Although completing the memo parts
may seem simple, how you complete the "To" and "From" may need
consideration. For example, it is fairly standard to address the recipient by
using the person's name and title and your own name and title as the
sender. Likewise, consider the subject or reference line carefully so that it
accurately represents the memo's contents. These details are important
especially if the memo is to be kept on file.

DATE: April 17, 1997

TO: Reid Anderson, Director of Clinical Services

FROM: Ira Pearlman, Clinical Associate *IP*

RE: HMO Reimbursement Policy

If you are sending the memo to more than one person and the group is
small (under ten people) you may wish to include all names of people
receiving the memo. Highlighting the individual recipient's name will help
that person to recognize immediately his or her connection to the memo.

Writer's Initials   The memo writer generally initials the memo next to his or her name in the
same way that the letter writer uses a signature to indicate that the work is
authorized.

FROM: Denice Bischoff, Clinical Associate   *DB*

Body of the Memo   Information in Chapter 7 addresses formats for writing effective memos.
Remember that short paragraphs, concise sentences, and lists can help to
make a memo easier to read. Be sure to organize your material in a useful
pattern.

*Standard typing format involves single-spaced paragraphs with double-
spacing between paragraphs.*

Reference Initials   In memos, reference initials are standard when letters are typed by a secretary.

The writer's initials appear in capitals followed by a colon or slash and the typist's initials in lowercase letters.

DLR:clf   *DLR/clf*

Reference initials are omitted if the writer is the typist.

In memos, the reference initials are seen less frequently since, with the advent of the personal computer, most often the writer of the memo is also the typist.

Enclosure Line

If you have enclosures that accompany your memo, you would indicate this by the word Enclosure or Enclosures or the abbreviation Enc. below the reference initials. You may also describe the enclosure.

Enclosure: Contract   *Enc.: Contract*

Copy Line

If copies of the memo are being sent to other readers, this can be indicated by the notation cc or c as desired. The colon is optional.

cc: Liz Zielinski   *c: Liz Zielinski*   *cc Liz Zielinski*

If a blind copy is being sent to a second reader, the notation bcc or bc is used. **NOTE:** The bcc or bc notation is placed on the copy of the memo that is sent to that person; however, it is NOT placed on the original memo. The recipient to whom the letter is addressed will not know that the bcc recipient exists.

Postscript

A postscript, usually indicated by P.S., is more common in personal letters than in business letters or memos. Avoid using postscripts too frequently. They may imply that the memo was poorly planned.

Second Page Memo Heading

The second and successive pages of a business memo should be indicated as such for identification purposes. This identification includes the name of the person being addressed, the page number, and the date. The information may be placed vertically or horizontally.

Ms. Courtney Frazer
Page 2
April 1, 1997

Ms. Courtney Frazer   *-2-*   *April 1, 1997*

If you can keep your memo to one page, please do so. More and more companies are advocating the one-page memo since conciseness is valued.

Example: Standard Memo Typing Style

NEW BEGINNINGS
FAMILY HEALTH CENTER

1027 Julidan Court
Collection Creek, Texas 45231

DATE: December 10, 1997
TO: Ellen White, Personnel Manager
FROM: Robert Rainer, Marketing Director *RR*
RE: Ad for Office Assistant Position

Your advertisement for the Office Assistant position will appear in *Info-Line* magazine on December 18. Please proof the attached ad carefully and let me know of any adjustments to format or style **prior to our December 15 deadline**. If the ad will require no adjustments, please fax it back to me (575-8900) as soon as you have approved it or before December 15.

I am available to answer any questions you might have and wish you the best of luck in your position search.

Enclosure

cc: Tim Sanderson

Practice Exercises to Supplement Chapter Concepts

CHAPTER 1: WRITING AS A PROCESS

Exercise 1-1: Prewriting

In response to the following scenarios attempt to prewrite by using one of the methods described in Chapter 1. While the scenarios focus on attempts at letter and memos, you should concentrate on how to prewrite the message. *An answer to the first item can be found in Appendix D.*

1. You need a new laser printer for your personal computer. Prewrite a memo to your supervisor indicating the volume of work that you perform that warrants the purchase, the condition of the current printer, and so on.

2. You must tell your assistant, Jocelyn Gerber, that she is being let go at the end of the month due to budget constraints. Prewrite this memo carefully.

3. You must request from your colleagues a donation to a charity that your company supports. Prewrite while considering the need to be persuasive.

4. The parking lot at your company will be repaved during the first week of March. You must notify all employees and provide alternate parking plans.

5. You have a client, James Patrick, whom you mistakenly overcharged during February for services rendered. Write to Mr. Patrick acknowledging and correcting the error.

Exercise 1-2: Revising & Editing

Revise the following letter so that it is more effective and professional. You may wish to alter the format (see Chapter 6).   Appendix B provides standard typing styles for letters. Also, edit for any typos or misspellings. *A revised and edited version of this letter is found in Appendix D.*

159 Pungon Lane
Boston, Massachusetts   56720

Ursula Leighton
1017 Melrose Drive
Portsmouth, Virginia   23510

January 4, 1997

Dear Ms. Leigton:

I regret to inform you that the position for which you applied, Administrative Assistant, was filled on January 3. Unfortunately, you were not selected. The employment committee reviewed over fifty applications before finalizing its decision.

I wish you the best of luck in your future employment endeavors.

Sincerly,

Shannon Spalding
Shannon Spalding, Office Manager

cc: Stephen Chapman

P. S. I will keep your resume on file should future opportunities arise.

CHAPTER 3: CONSIDER YOUR AUDIENCE

Exercise 3-1: Analyzing the Audience

When analyzing the audiences indicated below, refer to Figure 9 in Chapter 3: *Sample Questions for Writers to Ask.* Use the questions in Figure 9 to help you evaluate your audience. Possibilities will vary.

1. *Audience*: The mayor of your city; *Situation*: You are writing a letter to your mayor to inform him or her of your concern over a rezoning issue.

2. *Audience*: Elementary School Parent Teacher Association (PTA); *Situation*: You are writing a letter that will be read aloud at the next PTA meeting announcing your company's intention to be a corporate sponsor of the school.

3. *Audience*: Your supervisor; *Situation*: You are resigning over an irreconcilable difference with your supervisor yet wish to remain on good terms with this supervisor as well as with the administrators of your company.

CHAPTER 4: EVALUATE YOUR TONE

Exercises are found in Chapter 4 of the book with suggested answers in Appendix D.

CHAPTER 5: CREATE AN EFFECTIVE STYLE

Exercises are found in Chapter 5 of the book with suggested answers in Appendix D.

CHAPTER 6: WRITE EFFECTIVE LETTERS

Write a letter in response to each of the following situations. Refer to Chapter 6 for format and Appendix B for typing style as needed. The scenarios may provide information that you do not need to include in the letter. You must carefully evaluate the circumstances and plan and write the letter based on what you believe to be needed. You may create your own company title and address as appropriate. *A suggested letter written in response to the first situation can be found in Appendix D as an example.*

1. Recently you visited your local library with your ten-year-old daughter and became concerned at the noise level. Approximately ten other children of varying ages were talking and running in the library. During the one hour that you were there with your daughter who was trying to locate sources and take notes, the noise level continued to increase, making it extremely difficult for her to do her work. The librarian on call did not respond to your request to maintain order and a more respectful work atmosphere.

   Write a letter to the library director voicing your situation and requesting that general library rules be enforced. Address your letter to Marie Chlan, Library Director, Larigold Library, 714 Crescent Lane, Lansing, Michigan 33445.

2. You are the sales manager of a local hotel—Hanover Inn. The Montgomery Chapter of the Covert Management Society (CMS) hosted an annual one-day spring district meeting there. In making preliminary arrangements, the Hanover Inn agreed to

provide two suites for the officers (one for the international president and his wife and one for the district president and her husband) at a special price of $150 total.

The meeting was a success, and everything was fine until the final accounting from the Hanover Inn was sent to the Montgomery Chapter. The charge on the suites was $250, and there was also one long distance telephone charge of $12.65 billed to CMS which was made in the afternoon after the officers said they had checked out in the morning. The treasurer of the Montgomery Chapter, Betty Smith, appealed the two charges.

As sales manager of the local Hanover Inn, write a letter to Betty Smith admitting to the error and telling her to disregard the two incorrect charges (the additional $100 on the suites and the $12.65 for the phone call). You might remind her of the excellent facilities, good meals, and other reasons for the Montgomery Chapter to use the Hanover Inn in the future. Address your letter to Betty Smith, Treasurer, Covert Management Society, Montgomery Chapter, 1017 Matthew Way, Oviedo, Florida 44557.

3. You are the manager of the claims department in a small department store with a low volume of business. Therefore, it is the store's unwritten policy to grant few refunds and replacements on items returned 30 days after purchase. A customer, Frank Griffin, recently returned a sweater with which he was dissatisfied. The sweater which was red knit, size 42, contained a label that indicated that the sweater was wash and wear but must be washed by hand using a mild detergent. Mr. Griffin returned the sweater because after he had washed it in his washing machine, using the wash and wear cycle, the sweater would no longer fit. The sweater, now returned, is a size 40 instead of a 42. (He explained to you how he laundered it.) Mr. Griffin says the label said "wash and wear" so that the store should be accountable. The settlement wasn't made when he came into the store, but you said you'd respond in a couple days.

Write a letter to Mr. Griffin refusing the request for a refund or exchange because of the specific instructions on the label and because the garment was not properly laundered. However, you might provide an invitation to a special customer sale or a discount on another purchase. Write to Mr. Frank Griffin, 504 Courtney Drive, Lexington Park, Maryland 20657.

4. You are the personnel director of Anderson Associates. John Magee, the son of a friend, has applied for a sales associate job. Even though you like John and find him to be earnest in his desire to work well, he has no sales experience. Your advertisement stated a need for a minimum of two years' sales experience. Write a letter to John Magee letting him know that you are unable to consider him for the position. His address is 614 Lauren Lane, Lexington, Kentucky 56132.

5. You are graduating from college in two months. Write a letter to a former professor, Erika Lynch, asking her to write a letter of recommendation for you. Mention a specific job for which you are applying and let Professor Lynch know what the job title is and what skills the job requires. Give Professor Lynch the individual's name, title, and address to whom you are applying. Dr. Lynch's address is Old Dominion University, Office of Academic Affairs, Hampton Boulevard, Norfolk, Virginia 23529.

6. You have started a lawn care company to create part-time work during the summer. You provide mowing, weeding, planting, and general yard maintenance services. Write a sales letter and design a flyer as a package that you plan to mail to residents in your local community. Develop a company name and theme, standard rates for your services, background experience, and any other pertinent selling features.

7. You manage the shipping and receiving department of Claude Brothers, Inc., a manufacturer of electronic components that are used in brand-name computers. Two weeks ago, you shipped an order for 20,000 RD disk drives to one of your best customers. Yesterday, the sales manager brought you a letter from the customer explaining that all the 4X2 spindles that are part of the disk drives were not shipped and that you've gotten her in trouble with one of the firm's strongest clients. She asks that you not only ship the spindles by air express today, but that you also write the client explaining your responsibility for the problem. Write a letter to accompany the spindles that must be taken to the airport for a flight that departs three hours from now. In your letter, deliver the spindles, explain how the problem occurred (How did it occur?), accept responsibility, and explain what you've done to ensure that the problem will not recur. The client's name is Kim Nielson, Jameson Computer Company, 102 Sir Oliver Road, Annapolis, Maryland 80642.

8. You are the traffic control manager for Dominion Industries, an importer of Oriental rugs. Your company is located in the heart of the downtown business district, where it owns a parking lot adjacent to your main office building. Parking spaces in the downtown area are scarce and expensive, so Dominion Industries gives free parking privileges to all employees as a fringe benefit. Yesterday, you received a letter from Ginger Newark, the personnel director for Discount Department Store, located just three blocks away. Ms. Newark wants to know whether her store can rent a block of 25 parking spaces for its employees. If so, she will be glad to coordinate with you so you don't have to deal with 25 individual employees.

   Write a letter to Ms. Newark telling her that the spaces are available and that you will rent them as a block for an annual fee. Explain all the necessary details in the letter, including the price, and tell her that you are enclosing a contract for her signature. Her address is Discount Department Store, 1012 South Carroll Avenue, Michigan City, Indiana 34281.

9. You are interested in purchasing a Regent Classic SX 300 Television that is not available locally. Write to the Regent Company and request information about the specific television. Ask questions that you want answers to regarding price, guarantee, local availability, repair record, and so on. The address is 804 Rosebank Road, Eugene, Oregon 33982.

10. Judy Coldwater worked in your office at Communication Industries for seven months, under your supervision (you were office manager). On the basis of what she told you she could do, you started her off as a word processor. Her skills proved after three weeks to be inadequate, yet she seemed to be a hard worker. You decided to move her to accounts receivable. Again, she performed inadequately. She assured you that her real skill was in customer relations, so you moved her to the quality assurance department. After she spent three weeks making upset customers even angrier, you decided that Ms. Coldwater needed to be let go. You allowed her to resign before you would have to fire her.

Today you received a request from Ms. Coldwater for a letter of recommendation. She has applied for a position as a ticket agent for a travel company. You have no idea if she is qualified to do that type of work, and you don't feel you can do any more favors for Ms. Coldwater.

Write to Ms. Coldwater indicating that you have chosen not to write a letter recommending her for the sales job. Her address is 1029 Sam Circle, Richmond, Virginia 41523.

CHAPTER 7: WRITE EFFECTIVE MEMOS AND E-MAIL

Exercise 7-1: Traditional Memos and E-Mail

Write a memo in response to each of the following situations. Refer to Chapter 7 for format and Appendix B for typing style as needed. You must carefully evaluate the circumstances and plan and write the memo (traditional or e-mail) based on what you believe to be needed. You may create your own company title and address as appropriate. *A suggested memo written in response to the first situation can be found in Appendix D as an example.*

1. You attended a business meeting in Little Creek, Maine, and have to submit a travel memo detailing your expenses: airfare, $349; rental car, $169; hotel, $229; meals, $149. Send the memo to your supervisor Kim Sterling with a copy to Jane Danner, Assistant Controller.

2. A new engineer, Mr. Garrison Dale, has been hired by your department to begin work on March 9 at an annual salary of $54,000. As engineering department supervisor, write a memo to Glenda Humphreys, Director of Payroll Services, to notify her of Mr. Dale's appointment.

3. You are holding an annual retreat for all employees in your department. This one-day retreat will serve as a motivational, end-of-the-fiscal-year program. Sales have been lower this year than last, and morale is basically down. As director, write a memo to your employees informing them of the retreat program—date, time, and location. Enclose a copy of the program agenda for their reference.

4. You plan to be on vacation from June 16-27. Write a memo to a co-worker, Gail Bonner, whom you will be asking to check your messages during your absence and direct calls as needed. Propose a brief meeting to update Gail on any potential situations that might need her attention.

5. As director of the marketing department, you are holding the monthly meeting on December 4 to discuss new year advertising. Write a memo informing department employees of the meeting details and agenda.

6. For the past three years your office has provided employees with free one-day passes to Busch Gardens in Williamsburg, Virginia. This year due to low revenue, the office is unable to provide this benefit. As benefits manager, write a memo notifying employees that the passes will not be available this year.

7. Recycling bins were installed in the cafeteria of your building as well as in the outdoor garden area approximately one month ago. It has come to your attention that not all recyclable waste materials have been placed in the appropriate containers. As president of your agency, write a memo appealing to employees' desire to recycle materials appropriately.

8. Recently, your hospital went through an accreditation procedure by a national accrediting source. Due to employee dress code violations, your department was placed on probation for one month. As supervisor, write to your employees notifying them of the violations and the probationary period. Indicate your concern and notify the employees of an in-service mandatory training that will take place next week.

9. Your company has decided to institute a policy of mandatory random drug screening of employees. The policy will go into effect on July 14. Write a memo detailing how the policy will be implemented.

Exercise 7-2: Action Memo Format

1. Write an action memo in response to the following situation. Follow the format given in Chapter 7 to order your information.

    You are Training Coordinator for the Stealth Insurance Company. Your agency employs approximately 500 people. Due to recent budget constraints, the agency will need to downsize within the next 6 months by decreasing its number of employees to 400. The budget crisis has occurred as a result of excessive claims that have left the company in a financial deficit.

    In order to make the transition as smooth as possible, you will need to coordinate training sessions on "managing change" to help all employees manage the upcoming changes. Employees who are being cut as well as those who will remain will be impacted by the reduction in staff. These training sessions must be held within the next month.

    In order to hold an adequate number of effective training sessions, you must limit each session to a group of 25 employees. That means that you will need 20 training sessions to train all 500 staff members. You cannot train that many people yourself and have been given a budget of $8,000 to provide the necessary assistance. You could hire consultants to help you; however, the going rate per consultant is $1,000 per day. You could purchase a number of training videos on the topic for employees to view, but you believe a personal delivery would be measurably more effective with this particular group. If you attempted to deliver all of the workshops yourself, that would result in your doing one workshop per day which would be too time consuming given your busy schedule and varied responsibilities.

    The best option seems to be to train two other management employees to assist you in the delivery of the workshops. You can purchase a training package and use it to teach the two employees. After co-training for two sessions with you, these two employees would then be qualified to train separate groups. This method would free up your time and allow you to provide additional personal counseling time for a select group of key employees who have been with the agency the longest and would be most affected. Purchasing the training package would cost $1,000, and the cost of compensation for these two employees' time would be $3,000. The latter amount would cover the two employees' lost productivity from their regular positions. You estimate also that training folders and Xeroxed materials would cost $800. The total fee would be much less than $8,000. The added savings would allow you to purchase computer programs that could be used by downsized employees to rewrite their resumes for potential jobs. All in all, you think this idea is the best recommendation.

Write an action memo to your boss, Kathryn Elliott, Executive Director, informing her of your decision. Follow the specific action memo three-paragraph format given. Be sure to order the information according to the format.

2.   Write an action memo in response to the following situation. Follow the format given in Chapter 7 to order your information.

You are Public Relations Director of Flavin Realty. It is the end of the fiscal year, and you have been told that you have $1,000 to spend on equipment. You have needed a scanner in your office for some time since your ads have required higher quality images more recently than you have used in the past. In fact, the office has received negative feedback based on clients' dissatisfaction with fliers advertising their homes.

You have several alternatives. You have researched a scanner that is available for $900. This model includes software as a part of the price; however, you are not in need of the software. The problem with this option is that your current printer cannot handle the dpi resolution that this scanner would require. To purchase this scanner would require the need to purchase a new printer as well.

You could also purchase a scanner/printer/copier option that costs $700; however, the printer component of this machine works very slowly and would not be adequate for your level of work.

You have found a scanner/printer/copier option that is $1,000. This would provide the necessary printer with dpi resolution and would be fast enough for your purposes. It has the added feature of a copier in the event that your office copier is unavailable.

Write an action memo to your supervisor, Viola Flavin, President of Flavin Realty, informing her of your decision. Follow the specific action memo three-paragraph format given. Be sure to order the information according to the format.

CHAPTER 8: CHOOSING THE RIGHT WORD: PROPER USAGE

A usage exercise is found in Chapter 8 with correct answers in Appendix D.

CHAPTER 9: AVOIDING THE FIVE MAJOR GRAMMAR ERRORS

Exercises are found in Chapter 9 with suggested answers in Appendix D.

Suggested Answers to Exercises

CHAPTER 1: WRITING IS A PROCESS
(Exercises found in Appendix C)

Exercise 1-1: *While answers may vary, what follows are examples of possible brainstorming and outlining created in response to item 1.*

Brainstorming: New laser printer needed

Research the item

Compare prices

Cost of top two options

Volume of my work warranting need

Current printer condition and inadequacies

Recommended printer condition and options

Time saved with new printer

Increased work load possible with new printer

Diverse uses

New printer better for scanner dpi

Convince Sharon of advantages

Outlining:

- Discuss need for new printer
- Mention current printer condition and inadequacies
- Discuss increased volume of work warranting need for new printer
- Present research on market items
- Indicate top two items and costs
- Support worth of chosen item
- Present item's merits: capabilities
- Present item's compatibility with scanner
- Close with strongest support for purchasing new printer option

Exercise 1-2: Revising & Editing

The revised version reflects possible letterhead that might have been used for this example.

Spalding Enterprises
159 Pungon Lane
Boston, Massachusetts   56720

January 4, 1997

Ursula Leighton
1017 Melrose Drive
Portsmouth, Virginia   23510

Dear Ms. Leighton:

The Employment Committee met on January 2 to review applications for its current opening. Over fifty applicants applied for the position of administrative assistant; therefore, the decision required careful consideration.

While your application was appreciated, we felt that one individual better met our specific needs. We wish you the best of luck in your future employment endeavors and will keep your resume on file should additional positions open.

Sincerely,

Shannon Spalding

Shannon Spalding, Office Manager

cc: Stephen Chapman

CHAPTER 4: EVALUATE YOUR TONE
(Exercises found in Chapter 4)

Exercise 4-1:

1. Thank you for your letter of July 14 indicating that you have not received your order. We are sending a second order immediately.

2. We are happy to provide you with a second opportunity for a week's free advertising space. In fact, if you apply now, we will also provide (. . .continue with benefits of the offer).

3. Please complete your portion of the Anderson report, the directory information section, by Friday, August 4, at noon. That will allow me enough time to add it to the final report which is due out of the office on Monday, August 7. If you have any questions, please call me at 545-0110. Thanks.

Exercise 4-2:

1. Thank you for attending our banquet.

2. Your request to take vacation during December has been received. or
   I've received your vacation request for December.

3. Your new calculator is guaranteed for three years, so you can be sure you're getting a quality machine.

Exercise 4-3:

1. I have received your payment.

2. Your monthly statement indicates that payment must be made within ten days.

3. Following the instructions in the operator's manual (p. 9) for oiling the mechanism will ensure that your sewing machine performs at its optimum level.

4. If you reply immediately, we will be able to ship your equipment. or
   We will ship your equipment as soon as we hear from you.

5. I am referring to your April 17 letter about our weekly meeting.

6. I am unable to attend the meeting on December 23.

7. The interviewee who arrives on time will be treated with full consideration.

8. For the report to be delivered on time, all group members must submit their portions according to schedule. Unfortunately, the Beilo report will be late since one section was not submitted on time.

CHAPTER 5: CREATE AN EFFECTIVE STYLE
(Exercises found in Chapter 5)

Exercise 5-1:

1. Marcia Moore sent the memo three weeks ago.

2. Our assistant manager awarded the check to the hospital.

3. A stray dog bit the child on her left arm.

4. Matthew's teacher awarded Matthew the Science Merit award for his division. or His teacher awarded Matthew the Science Merit award for his division.

5. The neighbors on Main Street sent the new couple a "welcome basket."

Exercise 5-2:

1. Kamil frequently uses his charge account that he opened last year.

2. Despite her anticipation, Beatrice was annoyed as she read the report. or Anticipating a favorable response, Beatrice was annoyed as she read the report.

3. Parking is permitted by the attendant in the lot identified by the blue marker.

4. As a new employee, you will be provided training sessions by managers. or Managers will provide orientation sessions for new employees.

5. He ordered five dozen markers with pocket clips for his committee members.

CHAPTER 6: WRITE EFFECTIVE LETTERS
(Exercise found in Appendix C)

Exercise 6-1: *This is a possible letter response to the Exercise 6-1, item number 1.*

115 Orkney Drive
Lansing, Michigan   33445

May 1, 1997

Marie Chlan, Library Director
Larigold Library
714 Crescent Lane
Lansing, Michigan   33445

Dear Ms. Chlan:

On April 24 I visited the Larigold Library with my ten-year-old daughter Brianna to locate sources for a school project. While we normally find the Larigold Library conducive to study with a pleasant, quiet atmosphere, we did not find that to be so on that day. Approximately ten children of varying ages were disrupting the quiet atmosphere for all those present. I asked the on-duty librarian to maintain order; however, she did not respond to my request. My daughter and I decided to leave to find a more suitable work space.

I am writing to let you know my specific experience and to ask that you emphasize with patrons and workers the need to enforce general library rules. Since I have long enjoyed using the Larigold Library, I would greatly appreciate anything you might do to remedy this situation.

Sincerely,

Tiffany Sharp

Tiffany Sharp

CHAPTER 7: WRITE EFFECTIVE MEMOS AND E-MAIL

(Exercise found in Appendix C)

Exercise 7-1: *This is a possible memo response to the Exercise 7-1, item number 1.*

DATE: May 8, 1997

TO: Kim Sterling, Director
            Human Resources

FROM: Fontelle Kreuger, Assistant Director *FK*
            Human Resources

RE: Expenses in Travel to Little Creek, Maine

On May 1-4, 1997, I attended the Northern Regional Business Associates meeting in Little Creek, Maine. A detailed report regarding the meeting's decisions will be submitted on May 15 as we had agreed. Below is a report of my travel expenses with attached receipts.

<u>Travel Expenses</u>

Airfare	$349
Rental Car	$169
Hotel (3 nights @ $70 per night plus tax)	$229
Meals	<u>$149</u>
	$896

All receipts comply with the standards for local travel that Janice gave me. If you have any questions, please let me know.

Enclosures: Receipts
cc: Jane Danner, Assistant Controller

(Exercise found in Chapter 8)

Exercise 8-1:

1. accidentally
2. Who's
3. accept
4. a half, half a (either option is correct)
5. altogether
6. Your
7. already
8. advice
9. An, an
10. elude
11. among
12. assented
13. assure
14. device
15. Beside
16. than
17. burst
18. effected
19. affected
20. effects
21. May, dessert
22. can hardly
23. data
24. site
25. coarse
26. complimentary
27. conscious, conscience
28. couldn't care less (to mean that he could not care any less than he now cares) (Because this item sounds like a double negative even though it is technically correct, you may want to avoid it.)
29. is
30. are
31. could've
32. criterion
33. disinterested
34. Capitol
35. illicit
36. eminent
37. farther
38. fewer
39. well
40. have
41. themselves
42. implies
43. In regard to
44. Regardless
45. It's, its
46. teach
47. Let's, lose
48. may be
49. A lot
50. all right
51. moral
52. I (the meaning is "as I did")
53. passed
54. Personnel
55. phenomenon
56. principal, principles
57. quit, quite
58. said
59. stationary
60. then
61. They're, there
62. to, too
63. he
64. emigrated, immigrated
65. latter
66. adapted
67. sure to
68. broken
69. respectively
70. used to
71. morning
72. explicit
73. Almost
74. continual
75. discreet

CHAPTER 9: AVOIDING THE FIVE MAJOR GRAMMAR ERRORS
(Exercises found in Chapter 9)

Exercise 9-1: *The errors are identified and a sample revision follows for each example.*

1. Fragment. Believing that you will want an analysis of sales for November, we have sent you the figures.

2. Comma Splice. She asked me to research the latest standards for pricing; therefore, I did so quickly.

3. Fragment. He declared that such a procedure would not be practical and that it would be costly also.

4. Fused Sentence. This campaign will help sell Widener products. The outcome looks promising.

5. Fragment. Generally speaking, profits are at an all time high.

6. Comma Splice. A possible refund was recommended; however, it would go against policy.

7. Comma Splice. The new contract provides substantial wage increases; the original contract emphasized shorter hours.

8. Fragment. The flood damaged much of the equipment in Building 21. This made it necessary to stop production.

9. Correct.

10. Fused Sentence. The new model is being introduced this year; it is designed for the adventurous.

Exercise 9-2: *Agreement Errors. For each sentence, the subject and correct verb choice OR the antecedent and correct pronoun choice are indicated below.*

1. branches **stock**
2. existence **is**
3. fear **is**
4. "opportunities" **has**
5. definition **covers**
6. Nancy and Jim **have**
7. manager **has**
8. jack and hubcap **were**
9. one **is**
10. statue or plant **adorns**
11. problem **is**
12. one, **she**
13. cat, **its**
14. neither, **he/she is**
15. periodical, **its**
16. team, **its**
17. everybody, **his/her**
18. person, **he/she wants**
19. committee, **its**
20. secretaries, **they**

Exercise 9-3: *Gender Awareness. Sample revisions follow.*

1. Each employee must meet with his or her supervisor to discuss his or her performance appraisal.

   Preferred: All employees must meet with their supervisors to discuss their performance appraisals.

2. It is Nancy's job to staff the desk during the lunch break.

3. I do not think that worker's compensation will cover your medical bills.

4. Each manager should submit his or her monthly report.

   All managers must submit their monthly reports.

5. The chair of every committee at that university is involved in the planning process.

6. Dr. Thomas is our keynote speaker, and Ms. Spalding will provide our opening address.

   Andrew Thomas is our keynote speaker, and Victoria Spalding will provide our opening address.

7. According to the eighth grade teacher, each student will be given enough time to look over his or her material before taking the quiz.

   According to the eighth grade teacher, all students will be given enough time to look over their material before taking the quiz.

8. Every writer should be aware of his or her audience while beginning the writing process.

   All writers should be aware of their audiences while beginning the writing process.

9. Every businessperson will benefit from the rigorous exercises in the new book.

10. Extreme courage is required of every fire fighter.

APPENDIX A: GRAMMAR ASSISTANCE

(Exercises found in Appendix A)

Exercise A-1: *Identifying Grammar Terms*

1. Information
2. is provided
3. on, for, in
4. you
5. Wow!
6. and
7. effectively, carefully
8. inexpensive

Exercise A-2: *Comma Self Check*

1. Although Gary preferred Marie, Marvin was chosen.

2. That flag has green, yellow, and red stripes.

3. Bonita and Ahmad were both prepared to interview.

4. My grandparents' new address is Route 2, Box 39-B, Compton, Maryland 20650.

5. Preparing the department budget, as my boss has told me, will be quite time intensive.

6. The reason is that the dress is too elegant to wear.

7. The armed forces excelled on the ground and in the air.

8. Correct

9. The work may take two hours, or it may take only one hour.

10. Even with gloves on his hands and a hat on his head, he was still cold.

Table of Figures

Index

About the Author

Cynthia Bischoff has worked extensively as a business writing trainer, technical editor, and college English instructor since 1980. For the past eight years she has been employed at Old Dominion University as Director of the Center for Professional Training and Academic Development where she manages over 100 courses, workshops, and conferences per year. She also teaches credit courses in Effective Business Writing for the MBA Program, Management Writing for the English Department, and Effective Business Communications for the College of Engineering ACTE Program. Through the Center for Academic Television, she created a videotape series entitled *Professional Writing for Engineers* that is sold nationally. She has also taught three national television shows on business writing for National Technological University. According to evaluations of all television shows produced in 1996 by National Technological University—over 550 shows— Ms. Bischoff's evaluations for her television show **Business Writing That Works** ranked her in *the top ten best shows in the nation.* In addition, she has authored two composition textbooks for Houghton Mifflin Company of Boston.

Ms. Bischoff currently resides in Norfolk, Virginia, with her children, Matthew and Courtney, and her husband, Bruce. Her next book, **Essential Business Grammar Skills,** will be published in the fall of 1997. For further information or to purchase a copy, call 757-451-0741.

Ms. Bischoff teaches a variety of training workshops
on topics of business communications, including:

- Writing
- Editing
- Listening Skills
- Conflict Management
- Practical Meeting Skills
- Report Writing
- Interviewing Skills

Besides giving lectures open to the public, her
workshops can be held ON SITE for your agency.

For details, please call **757-451-0741** or **757-451-1417**.

To order additional copies of *Business Writing that Works!* fill out the coupon below.
Please allow 3-4 weeks for processing and shipping.
For questions or information on quantity discounts, call 757-451-0741.

BUSINESS WRITING *That Works!*

Qty	Title	Price Per Copy	Total Price
	Business Writing That Works!	$16.95	

Sorry, no credit cards. Make check or money order payable to Cynthia Bischoff.

Shipping and Handling $2.00 Per Book	
Order Total	

Name:

Company:

Address:

City: **State:**   **Zip:**

Phone: **Fax:**   **E-mail:**

Mail this coupon with payment to: White Raven Press • 115 Conway Ave. • Norfolk, VA 23505-4421

Coming soon!

in a limited edition
the companion volume to

BUSINESS WRITING THAT WORKS!

Essential Business Grammar Skills

by
Cynthia Bischoff

This book, based on Cynthia Bischoff's business grammar skills workshop, was designed for writers who requested an intensive review of grammar and punctuation.   Packed with tips, easy-to-follow rules, and clear examples, it will empower you to be a more effective and confident writer. For more information on ordering, please call 757-451-0741.

Name:

Company:

Address:

City: **State:**   **Zip:**

Phone: **Fax:**   **E-mail:**

☐ I would like more information on **Essential Business Grammar Skills** by Cynthia Bischoff.

☐ Please include my name on your mailing list for updates and for new products.

Mail this coupon to: White Raven Press • 115 Conway Ave. • Norfolk, VA 23505-4421

Pass along this extra copy to a friend.